Literacy Coaching

Developing Effective Teachers through Instructional Dialogue

Marilyn Duncan

Richard C. Owen Publishers, Inc.
Katonah, New York

Library of Congress Cataloging-in-Publication Data

Duncan, Marilyn.
    Literacy coaching: developing effective teachers through instructional dialogue / Marilyn Duncan
        p. cm.
    Summary: "Describes instructional dialogue, professional support in which a coach provides feedback to a teacher based on observation of and interaction in that teacher's classroom. Includes a DVD of classroom instruction and instructional dialogue between teacher and coach, focused on literacy"—Provided by publisher.
    Includes bibliographical references and index.
    ISBN-13: 978-1-57274-865-1 (pbk.)
    ISBN-10: 1-57274-865-6 (pbk.)
    1. Reading teachers—Training of.   I. Title.
    LB2844.1.R4D86 2006
    428.4'071—dc22

                                                                                    2006021928

Richard C. Owen Publishers, Inc.
PO Box 585
Katonah, NY 10536
914-232-3903; 914-232-3977 fax
www.RCOwen.com

Acquisitions Editor: Darcy H. Bradley
Copy Editor and Production Manager: Amy J. Finney
Production Assistant: Kathleen A. Martin
Design: Maryland Composition, Inc.

Printed in the United States of America

9   8   7   6   5   4   3   2   1

To my parents, Bob and Bette Lu Miller, who have always known—

- when to listen
- when to ask, and
- when to tell.

About *The Learning Network Solutions* Series

The resources in **The Learning Network® Solutions** series are based on the experiences of the educators involved with The Learning Network. The goal of the series is to offer:

- Practical books and tools **for** educators **by** educators
- Focused topics designed to address challenges in literacy education, classroom practice, or school development
- Concise explorations of the **what, how,** and **why** of a specific topic
- Accessible and conversational writing with useful, authentic examples.

About The Learning Network

Developed by innovative teachers and administrators, The Learning Network began as a dynamic design for increasing student achievement and improving schools. Since 1991, skillful staff developers have been building on this design to provide long-term job-embedded professional development, seminars, and other support in schools across the United States. As a result of this work, The Learning Network continues to evolve as a vigorous organization comprised of literacy coaches, teachers, administrators, and authors who work together to develop and implement educational solutions.

About *Literacy Coaching: Developing Effective Teachers through Instructional Dialogue*

Instructional dialogue is a key component of successful coaching and instructional leadership. It describes professional conversations that can occur between teachers and coaches in which the teacher is guided toward new learning and practice. This book provides information and support for implementing and sustaining the use of instructional dialogue in order to work more effectively with teachers.

TABLE OF CONTENTS

BEGINNINGS OF INSTRUCTIONAL DIALOGUE

Teachers are all too well aware that change is a real constant in their professional lives. For the most part, expectations for change have been about teaching practice. They are told it's better to teach this way rather than that way or that one instructional program is to be adopted instead of another. Yet probably the most profound expectations for change in recent years are to be found in the assumptions that underlie No Child Left Behind (Armbruster, Lehr, and Osborn 2001). To leave no child behind demands an emphasis on student learning as a measure of effective instructional practice.

Over many years I have been privileged to work with teachers and administrators who have always believed that the only measure of effective instruction is the extent to which it improves the learning of every student. In the early 1990s, I was introduced to The Learning Network®. This model of professional development includes a component for training site-based teacher leaders, who become teacher developers or coaches. Their training is from a Learning Network coordinator, who has developed expertise in the processes of teaching and learning, content standards, and working with adults. This model was years ahead of other professional development opportunities.

For me, the approach The Learning Network takes to professional development for teachers was a dramatic shift from what I had experienced earlier. Each school in The Learning Network assigns or chooses a minimum of two teacher leaders. The goal of training teacher leaders is to provide professional development that is job embedded; that focuses on improving student achievement by improving the effectiveness of classroom practice.

When working as a Learning Network coordinator, my colleagues and I developed a process for supporting coaches we called instructional dialogue. In effect, it was little more than a structured conversation that was a way of providing feedback and help for teachers to say more clearly what they were doing, why they were doing it, and how they might think about how they would change their practice to make their instruction more effective. The measure of this effectiveness was always student learning. The evidence was an increase in student achievement. Instructional dialogue proved challenging for many teachers. In an education culture that emphasized what to do and **how** to do it, it was disconcerting for many new teacher leaders or coaches to have a coordinator ask questions about what they were doing and **why** they were doing it. They felt that asking "why" was a suggestion that what they did was wrong or not good enough.

What I now understand is that teachers, like the students they instruct, are on a continuum of learning. There is no end point to learning for anyone at any time. The knowledge and skills teachers need are dependent upon the challenges they face with the next group of learners who walk into their classrooms.

This book describes a type of professional support that is meaningful and provides appropriate feedback to teachers that can make them more effective teachers. Developed over a period of fifteen years, instructional dialogue has become an important part of a teacher development process that can and does lead to improving the learning achievement of all students. To give the reader an idea about how instructional dialogue can work, this book includes a DVD showing an instructional dialogue between a teacher and a coach. This is intended to be one example of an instructional dialogue. In this case, it has taken place following a classroom observation. The style and approach will vary among different coaches and teachers. This footage illustrates one of the ways I have learned to work with teachers.

How to Use this Book

This book is divided into three parts. Part 1, Laying a Foundation for Reflective Teaching, is designed to answer the question, "**What** is instructional dialogue?" Introduced in Chapter 1 with a scenario of a teacher and coach working together, this provides the reader with an opportunity to see the process of instructional dialogue in action. Chapter 2 contains a definition of instructional dialogue, a description of how the process works, and an articulation of the roles of both the coach and the teacher involved in the process.

Part 2, Implementing a Process for Instructional Dialogue, is designed to support the reader in understanding **how** instructional dialogue works. Chapter 3 describes the action plan, a tool the teacher and coach use to determine the focus for the work they will do together. Chapter 4 explains the thinking of the coach as he or she works "on the job" with the teacher. Chapter 5 depicts the role of the coach during instructional dialogue. Chapter 6 puts the action plan, the job-embedded work, and instructional dialogue together in a description of the process that is depicted in the DVD that accompanies this book.

The book concludes with Part 3, Ensuring that the Process of Instructional Dialogue Works, which explores the **why** behind instructional dialogue. Chapter 7 describes the need for a school to develop agreements in order for the process to be transparent. Finally, Chapter 8 shares the research that supports the concept of instructional dialogue.

In one sense, this is a handbook; a book that is a reference for those supporting teachers as they develop as more competent professionals. But it's not a typical handbook. The difference is that this handbook is about people who are learning at different rates and in different ways, not things that are pre-programmed to work in particular ways if the right actions are taken. And one thing we know about adult people is that as diverse learners they learn more effectively when they learn together.

An underlying theme of this book is collegiality; the idea that a group of colleagues share responsibility toward achieving a common goal. This book supports the goal of developing teachers to become more confident, competent professional educators. It may work well for small groups of coaches and teachers to study this book and the accompanying DVD, try some of the suggested approaches for working together and instructional dialogue, and regroup periodically to share experiences. What is critical to this process is how the collegial environment supports adult learners, who when asked "why?" are often tentative and reluctant to expose themselves to the scrutiny of others. Since the need to work together is an essential component of this kind of professional learning, there is a real responsibility on the part of those who lead these group experiences to develop quickly the kind of respect and trust within the group that again is an underlying theme of this book. Whether study groups form as a district initiative, at the school level, or from small groups of colleagues simply wishing to work together, respect and trust are crucial to success.

To consider this handbook as a resource and a guide, that together with the kind of leadership in the local district or school that inspires colleagues to become better at what they do best, is how I would like to think *Literacy Coaching: Developing Effective Teachers through Instructional Dialogue* could be most helpful.

ACKNOWLEDGMENTS

The process of instructional dialogue is the result of an evolution of ideas. It began in the 1990s with the work of Jan Duncan in the training of teacher leaders and coordinators for The Learning Network® (TLN). This group of TLN coordinators worked in hundreds of schools across the United States and through that work refined their skills of dialogue. As a result, the coordinators were able to analyze and identify the qualities of effective instructional dialogue and link the results to increased teacher competence and student achievement. This book would not have been possible without the support of my colleagues. Special thanks go to my friend Dianne Kotaska for her continued thoughtful reflection on this process of teacher development.

In addition, I would like to thank the instructional coordinators, district coaches, and teacher leaders from Aurora Public Schools in Denver, Colorado, who have provided the opportunity for me to study the process of instructional dialogue at the district level. These professionals show a depth of commitment to the learning of teachers and students that is exemplary.

I owe a huge debt of gratitude to Jan Lasater, whose classroom was the kind of environment that drew me in and made me want to stay. Her willingness to share her reflection with others is a tribute to her as an educator.

The input from those who read this book prior to publication has been invaluable. It has made a huge difference in both organization and content. Thank you to Marsha Riddle Buly, Robert Low, Mary Catherine Moran, Shari Robinson, Richard Owen, and Jeanie Welch. Thanks to Darcy Bradley for being able to show me that writing is worth it–that after the hard work is the realization that each draft is better than the one before, to Amy J. Finney for quality control above and beyond the call of duty, and to Phyllis Morrison for always being there, no matter what.

Finally, to my husband Peter–I marvel in your ability to ask the kinds of questions that bring clarity to my thinking and my writing. Your personal encouragement has given me so much professional confidence. Thank you.

PART 1

Laying a Foundation for Reflective Teaching

CHAPTER **1** ___ A COACHING SCENARIO

esse is a classroom teacher in an urban elementary school. He has been working with me as his literacy coach for the past year. We have developed the kind of relationship over time that allows us to talk freely about the challenges Jesse faces in his teaching. Jesse writes action plans weekly that help him to talk about and uncover those current challenges. He knows that the action plans also help me determine the kind of support to use so that together we can help solve these challenges.

Jesse's current action plan has to do with the comprehension of his struggling readers. We have talked about this challenge and he has jotted down some of his thinking and what he is trying to do, as shown in Figure 1.1.

Jesse gives me his action plan before we meet, and I take some time to think about what I'm going to look for when I go into Jesse's classroom and how my support might look. I ask myself questions as I look at the action plan. What does Jesse already know about supporting readers struggling with comprehension? What are his strengths? What is he working on and what might he try next?

I know from the work I have done alongside Jesse that he has a good system for monitoring the progress of his readers. Jesse takes running records (Clay 2000) on the students who are struggling with reading on a monthly basis. Through coaching, we have worked on running record analysis over the past few months. I'm confident that running record analysis is a strength that Jesse has. I am also pleased to see his focus on comprehension. Previously, Jesse had concerns about the fact that his "proficient readers" were good at word-calling; they didn't really seem to understand what they were reading even though they were accurate readers.

ACTION PLAN

Name   Jesse   **Date**   January 19

What is your current challenge in literacy instruction?

The comprehension of my struggling readers is not improving as quickly as I'd like it to.

What is/are your question/questions?

How can I get these readers to stop when it doesn't make sense? How can I get them to try putting in words that make sense AND look right?

What do you know about that area, and what are you trying?

The running records that I have taken on these readers show me that they just put in any word that starts with the same letter (sometimes it even ends the same) but it makes no sense. They just keep on reading. I am trying to pick books for their reading groups that they are interested in and know something about so they have a reason to read.

What support do you need?

Could you watch me work with them? I've tried everything I can try so I'm out of ideas of what to do next.

Figure 1.1: Jesse's action plan

Jesse and I had worked to change his instruction. He was pleased with the result. The current assessments he administered with his proficient group of students showed a marked difference in their achievement, as demonstrated by their improved oral and written retellings and summaries. I write some reminder notes on his action plan (Figure 1.2). I write that another strength Jesse has is his understanding that proficiency in reading has everything to do with understanding what you read.

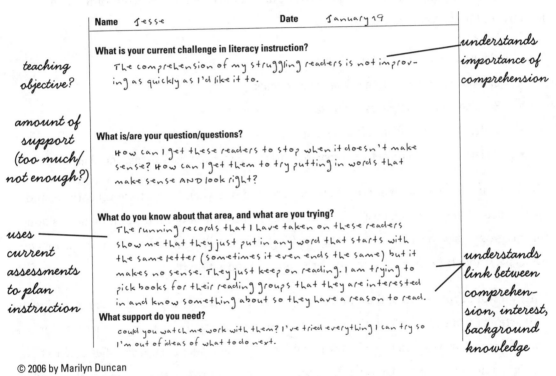

Figure 1.2: My notes on Jesse's action plan

I believe that Jesse's questions, "How can I get them to stop when it doesn't make sense?" and "How can I get them to substitute words that make sense and look right?" are right on target and very realistic. I wonder what his teaching objective for this struggling group is and jot down a note on his action plan to look at Jesse's planning. Jesse and I have worked on planning for instruction previously, so I know that he will not be concerned if I look at his teaching plan for this lesson.

I also make a note that Jesse is thinking about the kind of resources he is selecting for this group of students. In his action plan he says, "I am trying to pick books for their reading groups that they are interested in and know something about so they have a reason to read." This also confirms another strength that Jesse has. I write: "Understands the link between comprehension, interest, and background knowledge."

I have made these notes of Jesse's strengths:

- Current assessments used to plan for instruction
- Running record analysis is complete
- Understands importance of comprehension
- Understands the links between comprehension, interest, and background knowledge.

I have also made a few notes about what I need to find out when I'm in Jesse's classroom and when we're talking together. I want Jesse to share his thinking about the planning he has done for this group with me. I wonder: "Is the teaching objective directly linked to the behaviors he wants his students to change?" I make a brief note on the action plan.

Finally, I will be interested in the amount of support I see Jesse giving these students during the instruction. I wonder if the questions Jesse asks are supporting the learning of these students. I know from my own experience of working with struggling readers that it's challenging to find the right amount of support and it's often tempting to support too much. I decide that I will listen to both the questions Jesse asks his students and to the students' responses. By noting both the questions and responses I should be able to help Jesse reflect on the learning that is occurring as a result of his teaching. I make some final notes: "Amount of support–evidence of learning: too much or not enough?"

Jesse and I have scheduled a time for our work together. When I come into the classroom, Jesse is working with an individual student. He tells me he's nearly finished and asks if I'd like to see his plan for today's lesson. He hands me a clipboard with his planning sheet attached. I read the objective for today: "To comprehend what is being read." I know that for Jesse and these students that is the overall outcome, but I'm wondering if that objective might be too broad for this lesson. I remember a question Jesse asked in his action plan: "How can I get them to stop when it doesn't make sense?"

I see that the resource Jesse has selected is a three-page piece entitled "Sounds in Space" (O'Brien 1988) from an anthology. Space is a science topic that the class has been studying. I note that while this short piece of writing is expository, the illustrations are cartoon-like, which could pose an interesting challenge to the students. Jesse finishes his work with the individual student and takes a quick walk around the classroom to make certain that the other students are able to continue working independently. He calls the small group to the table.

Jesse begins by asking the students to look at the first page of the piece and think about what the piece is going to be about. Underneath the title and author name and surrounding the illustration of planets and a rocket ship on the first page are the blown-up words ZAP! ROAR! BOOM! One of the students comments on these words while another student begins to talk about the rockets and aliens and space invaders that he saw in a cartoon the day before. A lively discussion begins about cartoons that are about space. Jesse listens for a bit, then asks the students to think about the title of the piece. He asks the group if thinking about the title made them think differently about what they were going to read. One student mentions that it's probably about sounds and wonders what that would have to do with aliens. Jesse wonders aloud if the piece is fiction or nonfiction. There's disagreement among the group, some saying that the illustrations make them think about fiction; others saying the title makes them think it's nonfiction. Jesse says they probably need to get started. He asks them to read and to stop if they come to any words that they don't know. There is a high level of enthusiasm among the students for what they are going to read.

I have taken some notes during the instruction. I have written down what Jesse has said and the student responses. I also jotted a few notes to myself: "Questions that focus on meaning– questions that focus on words."

The students begin to read, and most of the conversation as they read is about the words they are trying to figure out. Throughout the lesson I continue to write down Jesse's questions and the students' responses. Jesse finishes the instruction and we confirm our time for instructional dialogue.

I spend a few minutes preparing for the dialogue by thinking about the lesson I observed. I think about the strength in Jesse's instruction and put a few stars next to places where I noted that Jesse really focused on comprehension. I jot down some questions: "What did you want them to learn? Were they successful? How do you know?" I know that Jesse has an outcome for his students. He wants them to increase their comprehension skills. But I am wondering how I can help Jesse plan for this to happen during the lesson. I write down another question: "When does comprehension occur?"

I have some ideas about how to help Jesse think about his teaching during the dialogue, but I also know that the outcome of the dialogue is going to depend upon what Jesse says during our conversation. I bring some professional books on the reading process in case we want to refer to them. Since we will meet in Jesse's classroom for the dialogue, I also know that his student assessments and his teaching plans will be available as a resource as well.

Later in the day, Jesse and I meet for our instructional dialogue. The instructional dialogue provides the opportunity for us to reflect on the lesson. Jesse articulated a challenge through his action plan. He asked me to support him, in this instance, by observing his teaching. Jesse expects that the structured conversation we have as our instructional dialogue will help him overcome the challenge he has with the struggling readers. We begin.

Marilyn:	How do you think it went today?
Jesse:	It was a little better than some of the other lessons, but I think I might have picked a piece with too many hard words.
Marilyn:	Why do you say that?
Jesse:	There seemed to be a lot of words they couldn't read.

Marilyn: Let's go back to your action plan. What seems to be the challenge right now?

Jesse: This group of kids does not comprehend like I want them to.

Marilyn: So what would it look like if they comprehended well?

Jesse: They would know what the text is about and be able to talk about it. They would be able to get past some of the problems they have with words because they would be thinking about the whole thing.

Marilyn: Absolutely! So let's think about what you did to support that kind of reading. You did a really good job of focusing on meaning before they started reading. Do you remember what you did?

Jesse: I asked them to look at the first page and see if it gave them an idea of what the book would be about. I thought they would like this piece because it was about space and also because of the cartoon-type illustrations.

Marilyn: Those were two really great reasons for picking the text. Could you see that they were interested in this piece?

Jesse: Yes. There was a lot of enthusiasm. Most of the kids did a lot of talking. That's what frustrates me. It seems to start out really well and then it tends to fall flat.

Marilyn: Let's think about the kinds of questions you posed that seemed to generate that rich discussion. Do you remember any of them?

Jesse: Not really.

Marilyn: Your first question that focused on the page and their predictions generated all of that discussion about aliens and rockets.

Jesse: Yes. I thought I was going to lose them for a second on that one. I could hear us talking for the next twenty minutes about the after-school cartoons.

Marilyn: So it was a smart move for you to ask the next question. You said, "Look at the title of this piece. What does that make you think about?"

Jesse: I was shocked when Desiree read the title and immediately said that she thought it had something to do with sounds because of the *Boom! Roar! Zap!* See, that's what I don't get. Why was it so easy for her to read those words and not be able to read other words in the text?

Marilyn: What helped her?

Jesse: The title, I guess, and the format of the illustrations. These kids do like comic books.

Marilyn: So your question about the title and your focus on the first page helped her make the kind of meaning that enabled her to make sense of some potentially "unknown" words.

Jesse: All that from a question? (laughs)

Marilyn: Then you made them think even deeper.

Jesse: That's when I asked them if they thought it was fiction or nonfiction. I loved that discussion. It actually sounded like some of the discussions my more proficient kids have.

Marilyn: It was really apparent the work you have done with them in identifying expository text. They were able to justify the reasons for their choices easily. So, let's think about the work you did to that point. Listen to those questions again: "What does the first page make you think this piece will be about? Look at the title of this piece. What does that make you think it will be about? Do you think it will be fiction or nonfiction?" What were all of those questions based upon?

Jesse: They were all about meaning.

Marilyn: And they resulted in your kids talking about meaning—in other words, comprehension.

Jesse: So what happened?

Marilyn: Listen to what you said next. "We'd better get started. Read the first page and stop if you come to any words that you don't know." What was that question based upon?

Jesse: It was more about words and not about meaning, wasn't it? It's not really what I meant.

Marilyn: What do you think the kids thought you meant?

Jesse: Probably that the words were going to be a problem. And they were.

Marilyn: So let's go back to where you were before you told them to read. What did you want them to find out when they finished reading that page?

Jesse: I wanted them to figure out if it was fiction or nonfiction.

Marilyn: Did they know that?

Jesse: Nope–aughh . . . I guess I have to figure out what I want them to comprehend, don't I? Not what words to be stuck on.

Marilyn: Why don't you take a minute and jot down some notes for yourself? (Jesse writes, "My prompt for reading has to be based on the meaning I want them to make.") So what would it sound like if you were prompting for meaning?

Jesse: In this case I could have simply said, "Why don't you read to find out whether this piece is fiction or nonfiction."

Marilyn: There you go–why would that be important?

Jesse: It would have given them a reason to read. The message I sent was that it was going to be too hard.

Marilyn: So when they came to the end of page 1, they should have been able to answer their question–fiction or nonfiction–and I would have expected them to have another question.

Jesse: It's right there in the last two sentences. "Space is never noisy. And there is a very good reason why." I would have wanted them to find out–why is space never noisy?

Marilyn: On that second page, would there have been some challenges with words?

Jesse: I'm pretty sure that *vibrate* would have been a tough one at the beginning. In fact, it **was** hard for them.

Marilyn: So what could you have done to help them with that one?

Jesse: The illustration is terrific. It shows sound waves. So even if we had had some discussion about the picture beforehand they would have at least gotten the idea.

Marilyn: And in that case, if the discussion doesn't reveal the word that's in the text, you can tell them that word. "So you have identified those waves in the picture as sound waves. Do you know another word for sound waves? It's a scientific word." And if no one had it, I'd say, "That word is *vibrate*. See if you can find the word *vibrate* on this page." Then we'd probably have a conversation about the difference between the words on the page that were derivations of *vibrate–vibration, vibrates*.

Jesse: I've never thought of having those kinds of conversations before we read the page. It makes so much sense.

Marilyn: Let's go back to what you said before. "My prompt for the reading has to be based on the meaning I want them to make."

Jesse: But this time the prompt involves words that will help them make meaning.

Marilyn: Yes! So let's look at how you planned for this lesson.

Jesse: I can tell you without looking. I planned by picking the objective and by picking the book. But that wasn't enough.

Marilyn: What do you mean?

Jesse: I need to plan for meaning making. I need to plan what I want to occur as they read so they can comprehend more effectively.

Marilyn: You might want to write that down.

Jesse: So my next focus needs to be on planning my instruction. Is that going to take me more time?

Marilyn:	It may initially, but I think you'll be able to do it more quickly as you work through it. Maybe that's what we should work on next week–planning some small group lessons.
Jesse:	That would help me.
Marilyn:	Before we quit, I'd like to see if we can make a few more links to what you're thinking about now. Where were the places you think your lesson was most effective today?
Jesse:	Well, definitely at the beginning–and I also think at the end because we talked about why there were no sounds in space.
Marilyn:	So you talked about the meaning at the beginning and the end, but what happened in the middle?
Jesse:	We only talked about the words they didn't know.
Marilyn:	When do we comprehend?
Jesse:	Not just at the beginning and the end (laughs). We comprehend the whole time we read.
Marilyn:	So how does that impact our planning?
Jesse:	Well, we have to plan for comprehension during the whole lesson–not just at the beginning and at the end.
Marilyn:	Excellent–you might want to write that down. (Jesse writes, "Comprehension occurs the whole time we read. I can plan for comprehension throughout the text.") Earlier you described what your kids will look like when they comprehend what they read. You said, "They would know what the text is about and be able to talk about it. They would be able to get past some of the problems they have with words because they would be thinking about the whole thing." So how will your planning lead your students to that kind of success?
Jesse:	I think I will be able to say to myself when I'm planning for comprehension, "What do I want them to get out of this page–or these pages? Are there any words that might get in the way?"

Marilyn:	Is it only words that might get in the way of comprehension?
Jesse:	No. Phrases could get in the way or even ideas, like not having the background knowledge or vocabulary. So I have to ask myself, "What could possibly get in the way of their comprehension, and how can I plan for that?"
Marilyn:	And sometimes those challenges are what you want to have in the text so that you can see that they (pointing back to Jesse's action plan) "Stop when it doesn't make sense" or "Put in a word that makes sense **and** looks right."
Jesse:	So my planning will help them develop the skills to **do** something about it if it doesn't make sense. That sounds like a lot of work to me! (smiles)
Marilyn:	That's why it's a good action plan for next week. So we can see how efficiently and effectively you can plan for this kind of instruction.

Jesse and I worked together over the next few weeks to plan specifically for the comprehension of his struggling readers. Because he was becoming more skilled in the selection of texts for these students, he found the planning to be less time consuming than he expected. He used self-stick notes to record his thinking for the support he'd need to provide throughout the text. He soon found that he had to expect more independence from these students than he had previously. He had to help these learners do more of the thinking before and while they were reading in order to help them overcome the challenges they might have been stumped by previously.

Jesse was pleased with the results. His next round of running records showed these students were, at the least, employing strategies that were supporting their ability to make meaning. He found that all but one student increased their reading levels in that month and a few students grew two levels or more. Most important was Jesse's increased knowledge and skill of how to plan more effectively for focused instruction and student learning, which had an impact on the student achievement of his entire class.

This coaching scenario was written as an overview of a process that we call instructional dialogue. Seeing the whole process at the beginning of this book should provide you with a picture of what instructional dialogue is. My hope is that it will make you wonder how the coach supports the development of the action plan, how the coach and the teacher decide on the kind of support needed, and about what strategies a coach needs to conduct the kind of instructional dialogue that not only results in new learning for the teacher but in increased achievement for the students as well. Chapter 2 explores more about what instructional dialogue is.

CHAPTER 2

DEVELOPING A PROCESS FOR INSTRUCTIONAL DIALOGUE

Instructional dialogue is a structured conversation about teaching and learning with a goal of providing feedback to the teacher. The measure of improvement is always student learning. An instructional dialogue is neither an interrogation nor a therapy session. It is a dialogue between colleagues learning from each other to do their jobs better. Instructional dialogue is an opportunity for teachers through the mentorship and facilitation of a coach to think about their practice and ways to improve it.

Instructional dialogue is also a process of professional development. The teacher, with the support of the coach, identifies a challenge to instruction through the vehicle of an action plan. This plan is the teacher's commitment to action. Together the teacher and coach determine how they will work together and gain information to provide quality feedback to the teacher. After the coach works alongside the teacher, they meet for a dialogue. The teacher commits to a change in classroom practice as a result of the dialogue. The impact of this change is expected to be evident through increased student achievement. Student achievement increases are measured by district, school, and classroom summative and formative assessments.

The process includes:

- A teacher's action plan setting out a current challenge with instruction
- The coach working with the teacher–this enables the coach to see the teacher in action and provide feedback
- An instructional dialogue that follows their work together

- A commitment to change by the teacher and a clear understanding about how this change in instruction will impact student learning

- A plan to follow up on the commitment to confirm successes or clarify confusions.

Remember Jesse's action plan in the previous chapter of this book? It uncovered the challenge he was having with his struggling readers. Because of the nature of his challenge, I was able to see Jesse in action as he was instructing these students in a small group. Where you see the teacher in action is dependent upon where his or her challenge lies. It could be learning how to use a new assessment tool, planning for instruction, or interacting with the whole group, small groups, or individuals. In Jesse's classroom, I was collecting information about his questions and the responses of his students in order to give him feedback that would help solve his challenge.

When I talk about feedback, I mean the opportunity for the teacher to reflect on his or her own practices with support from a colleague with more expertise—the coach. The instructional dialogue—the structured conversation—is where the reflection occurs. It results in a commitment to change by the teacher and some concrete strategies on how to implement that change. One of those strategies will be the collection of data that will show the impact of that change on student learning. The commitment to change will lead into the teacher's next action plan, providing opportunity for the teacher to confirm successes or clarify confusions in a timely manner.

Developing a Relationship between the Teacher and the Coach

"The foundation of a trusting relationship is believing that the other person has integrity. This is demonstrated by meeting commitments and keeping promises" (Kouzes and Posner 2002). Working together in instructional dialogue brings a new dimension to the professional relationships between teachers and a coach. Expectations change. There is a shift from simply being congenial to becoming collegial. Congenial conversations tend to be more about the surface-level practice of the job; collegial conversations are about sharing common professional values and interests. As conversations become more collegial, colleagues learn from one another to do their jobs better.

Successful coaches develop relationships with the people they support based on mutual respect and trust. Coaches operate at the height of professionalism. They are honest with the teachers they support. They talk **to** their colleagues, not about their colleagues. Teachers learn more from coaches who are trustworthy. It is beneficial, prior to beginning a coaching initiative, to articulate and clarify the roles and responsibilities of both the coach and the teacher. If teachers and coaches are clear about what can be expected of them and the commitments they make to each other, the relationship is off to a positive start.

Instructional dialogue operates on the belief that all teachers have strengths upon which they can build. By starting with what the teacher can do, the coach starts with the familiar. Respect comes when the teacher receives help solving their instructional challenges with the coach's expertise.

The work of the coach alongside the teacher is not part of the teacher evaluation system. Discussions and decisions during coaching are based on a continuum of growth for every teacher, so they are not about what the teacher is doing correctly or incorrectly. Information that is shared with the building administrator is about the teacher's progress along this continuum of growth. The teacher always knows what is being shared with the principal. The coach is not part of traditional teacher evaluation procedures.

Roles and Responsibilities for Instructional Dialogue

Teachers feel more confident about the coach's work when the structures leading to successful instructional dialogue are clear. Clarifying roles and responsibilities will allow the teacher's basic questions to be answered. What is the purpose of an action plan? What will the coach do with it? What will the coach do when we work together? What is instructional dialogue? What am I supposed to do and what will the coach do during the dialogue? How do I know this will be a productive use of time for me?

The Action Plan

The action plan is a tool for reflection for the teacher (Figure 2.1). The first question–What is your current challenge in literacy instruction?–encourages teachers to identify their current

ACTION PLAN

Name   **Date**

What is your current challenge in literacy instruction?

What is/are your question/questions?

What do you know about that area, and what are you trying?

What support do you need?

Figure 2.1: An action plan

instructional challenges. The next question–What is/are your question/questions?–asks teachers to narrow the challenge to the most pressing questions. The third question–What do you know about that area, and what are you trying?–allows the teacher to identify what they know and what they have tried to do to overcome the challenge. The final question–What support do you need?–asks the teacher to identify the kind of support they would like from the coach.

The action plan is also a tool to focus the support provided by the coach. It allows the coach to see where the teacher needs feedback. It provides the coach with a window into what the teacher already knows and has tried. It becomes a planning tool for their job-embedded work.

The teacher's role in using the action plan is to:

- Determine the current instructional challenge based upon the achievement of his or her students
- Ask questions about that challenge
- Describe what he or she currently knows and what he or she is doing about it
- Identify where he or she can work with the coach to receive the most helpful feedback.

The coach's role is to:

- Review and determine the best way to provide feedback to the teacher
- Plan how to provide support with input from the teacher.

Chapter 3 provides more detail about the process of using the action plan.

Job-embedded Work

The action plan assists the teacher in identifying the kind of support he or she needs to solve the current instructional challenge. Together the coach and the teacher determine what their job-embedded work will look and sound like. This work might find the coach demonstrating an assessment tool or instructional approach for the teacher. It might manifest as the coach working alongside the teacher to evaluate student work or conduct small group instruction. The coach might be watching the teacher work with the whole group, small groups, or individuals. The approach the coach uses to support the teacher is dependent upon the amount of assistance the individual teacher needs. Chapter 4 provides a more detailed explanation of how the coach prepares for work alongside the teacher.

The role of the teacher in the job-embedded work with the coach is to:

- Be prepared for the work time with the coach
- Be willing to ask for help when it's needed.

The role of the coach when working alongside the teacher is to:

- Stay focused on the teacher's question
- Collect information to support the teacher's work
- Ask questions that will allow both of them to best help the teacher reflect on practice.

Instructional Dialogue

The coach and teacher set aside time to have a conversation about the work the teacher has been doing and the work they have done together. This instructional dialogue is between fifteen and twenty minutes long. As a result of the dialogue, the teacher should have ideas for addressing his or her current challenge. The work during instructional dialogue is practical. The teacher has time to talk about what he or she has been doing. The coach listens, asks questions, and gives suggestions when needed. The dialogue provides the teacher with a plan for what to do next and strategies for how it might look and sound in practice. The coach and teacher will also discuss how this strategy will impact student learning. The teacher leaves the dialogue with a commitment to action—what he or she will do next. This includes collecting student work in order to confirm an impact on learning. This commitment will naturally lead into the next action plan. The coach's role in instructional dialogue is discussed in depth in Chapter 5.

The role of the teacher during instructional dialogue is to:

- Talk about his or her current action to solve the instructional challenges
- Analyze student work to determine the impact of his or her current action
- Determine what he or she will do next

- Determine why it should be effective (what is the understanding or knowledge behind the decision)

- Ask for support in how to implement the new strategy.

The role of the coach during instructional dialogue is to:
- Have an outcome for the dialogue and a plan for the support to be provided
- Listen carefully to what the teacher says
- Analyze student work
- Help the teacher set expectations for what he or she will do next
- Provide support, when needed, as to how this might look.

The purpose of the coaching experience is to develop the competence and confidence of teachers to meet the needs of the range of diverse learners in their classrooms. As a result of coaching, teachers become more reflective about their work as they work. By reflective I mean that they are thinking about their teaching as they teach and making changes along the way based upon student responses. Teachers' questions arise from their own instructional practice based on how effectively they raise student achievement. They are able to talk about what they are doing in their classrooms and why they are doing it. The success of this process rests on what the coach knows and is able to do. The next three chapters provide detailed descriptions of the skills a coach needs as a teacher developer.

PART 2:
Implementing a Process for Instructional Dialogue

CHAPTER 3   USING THE ACTION PLAN

This chapter looks more closely at the role of the coach and how the action plan helps to reveal what the teacher knows, what the teacher is coming to know, and what the teacher needs to know next. The chapter also considers how this information is used to plan for work alongside the teacher to provide the most useful feedback.

Teachers meet a new group of students each year. Because of social, economic, and cultural changes in the community, these students come to school with increasingly diverse needs. Teachers have to make decisions all the time about the diverse learners in their classrooms. Because the learners are disparate and the decisions are constant, teaching is a profession that is always changing. Change is a given. The job of teachers is to continually collect assessment data about each student and bring the knowledge and skills they have to evaluate that data. Based on the evaluated data they make instructional decisions on a minute-by-minute basis in the context of their instructional planning. Student achievement is dependent upon high-quality decisions.

Teachers are faced with instructional challenges on a daily basis. Coaching can become the support mechanism to help teachers overcome these challenges to instruction. Research reminds us that teachers who assess their own professional-development needs make choices about their learning. Through this assessment, teachers recognize the gap between what they want to know and are able to do and their current level of knowledge and skill. Of equal importance is how the teachers choose to close the gap and gain the knowledge and skills they need (Sadler 1989). Identifying the challenges of their instruction through the lens of student learning gives both the teacher and the coach a chance to open up their current knowledge to inquiry. The teachers will be thinking about their jobs on the job (Schön 1983).

The Learning Network®

ACTION PLAN

Name _____ School _____

Teacher ☐   Teacher Leader ☐   Administrator ☐   Other ☐   Date _____

What area do I need to explore?

What do I know about this area?

What questions do I have?

What question do I need to explore to develop my understandings?

How will I develop these understandings?
In my practice?

In other ways?

© 1999 by Richard C. Owen Publishers, Inc. 8/10/99

Figure 3.1: The Learning Network® action plan

For an action plan to be of benefit to both the teacher and the coach, it should provide opportunities for self-assessment and choice. As mentioned in Chapter 2, a quality action plan sets the stage for the coach's observation and the teacher's reflection. It should focus on:

- The teacher's current challenge in instruction based on student learning
- The questions the teacher has about that challenge
- What the teacher is already doing, and
- The support that would help the teacher overcome the challenge.

A supportive action plan is simple and jargon free. It is helpful for a school to personalize the design of an action plan to meet their needs, keeping in mind the components described above. The form should follow the process. If the teachers who are supported by a coach can't figure out how to use the form, the form is the problem, not the teacher. Figure 3.1 shows an example of a slightly different action plan.

Building on Strengths

All teachers bring strengths to their work. Coaches look for those strengths and build upon them. When looking for a teacher's strengths, the coach is not evaluating the teacher's work in a traditional sense. The coach is mindful of the root word of evaluation–value–and is looking for the teacher's current knowledge and skills to build upon as that teacher grows and learns.

A coach can use the essential characteristics of effective teachers (Allington 2002; Darling-Hammond 1998; National Board for Professional Teaching Standards; National Education Association 2003; Pressley et al. 2001; Pressley et al. 2003; Rényi 1996; Stronge 2002) to reflect on the strengths seen in each teacher. The characteristics provide a set of useful criteria for identifying teachers' strengths. A coach might consider if the teachers have:

- High expectations about their own learning and their students' learning
- Relevant information about their students
- Sufficient knowledge of content standards and process to evaluate the information about their students

- The skills to organize the classroom environment for student learning

- The skills to manage the learning of their students

- The skills to provide support for learning through whole group, small group, and individual instruction.

When coaches get a general sense of what teachers can do, then it becomes much easier to see what to do next.

Finding the Focus for the Action Plan

Conversations about student learning can help teachers uncover challenges to their instruction. One way challenges arise is when the whole school analyzes summative achievement data. As an example, one school's summative data showed that on the statewide test, the students in the school scored particularly well when comprehending literary text. But overall, the school's scores on comprehension of expository text were much lower. The presentation of this data caused the staff to ask themselves: "What do we need to know about teaching expository text that we don't currently know?"

The staff broke into small groups and looked at the kinds of texts and questions students were expected to respond to on the statewide test. They also looked at the state standards and the expectations that were stated for students when reading and writing expository text. In small groups they brainstormed their questions. Some of the questions they posed were:

- Do we understand the different forms of expository texts ourselves?

- Do our students know how to use text features to help them make meaning when they read?

- Do we know the skills our students need to read expository text?

- How much are we exposing our students to nonfiction texts?

- Do our classroom libraries and resource room contain sufficient expository texts?

The staff then broke into grade-level groups to think about the impact this challenge had on the stage of development of the readers they taught. Teachers in the early grades were in agreement that most of the texts used with their students were fiction or narrative texts. Conversations in the upper grades focused on the fact that for reading instruction, they were primarily using fiction. Because of the staff's analysis of the summative data, they saw a need to shift their professional development focus. Students were not achieving at the levels expected when comprehending expository texts. Teachers realized they were not using expository texts effectively in instruction. Professional development in the school would work toward developing readers who comprehend expository text. The staff agreed to come back to this topic periodically, with student assessments showing the impact their work was having on increased student comprehension.

This staff conversation naturally spilled into the development of teachers' action plans. Some grade-level groups left the meeting with a new action plan. Other individuals asked for support from their coaches in developing an action plan in this area. The literacy coaches in the school noticed an increase in the number of action plans that focused on understanding how to improve comprehension of expository texts.

The impact on student achievement was seen very quickly. The students were highly engaged in the opportunity to read more expository texts. The teachers were using expository texts in monthly assessments where previously they had only used narrative fiction. By the end of the second quarter of the school year, the teachers had a much better indication of the levels of comprehension in both literary and expository texts. The state assessment at the end of the year showed a marked increase in achievement of students at those testing grades.

Coaches have to keep the end in mind in regard to student learning. An effective coach knows what student proficiency looks like at each grade level. A coach also knows the kind of instruction that will support proficiency and the small steps that the teacher will need to take along the way. Each small step becomes an action plan.

Analysis of an Action Plan: An Example

The literacy coach is selected for the job because of a certain level of expertise in his or her knowledge about literacy. As stated previously, the coach is not evaluating the teacher in the traditional sense, but is placing a value on what the teacher can do in order to uncover what the teacher needs to do next to solve instructional challenges. The action plan is a tool that begins the reflective process for the teacher. It is also a tool for the coach to determine the kind of support the teacher wants and needs. Because of this, it's helpful for the coach to see the teacher's action plan prior to providing support. This allows the coach to plan for the instructional dialogue.

The coach has four questions in mind when looking at the action plan:

- *What does this information tell me about what the teacher knows?* This question allows the coach to identify the strengths that can be built upon.

- *What is the teacher trying to do in instruction?* This question can help the coach determine where the teacher is approximating.

- *What do I know about the teacher's challenge to improving student learning?* This question invites the coach to think about his or her own knowledge and skill and what he or she understands about the challenge the teacher is facing. The coach looks closely at both student learning and teacher learning.

- *What might the teacher need to learn next?* This question is based on the strengths the coach has identified, what the teacher is doing, and the coach's own knowledge. The action plan should lead the coach to an idea of what the teacher's next learning step might be.

When I receive an action plan prior to my work with a teacher, I read through it and ask myself the four questions above. I usually write my thinking on the action plan itself and often share these notes with the teacher during our instructional dialogue. Figure 3.2 shows Dennis' action plan. The following is how I analyzed it.

What does this action plan tell me about what Dennis already knows? I look at Dennis's statements based on what I already know about his instruction and on what he's telling me today. Dennis's action plan is about selecting appropriate books for small group reading instruction.

> This tells me that Dennis knows that the same text will not meet the needs of all learners.

His questions also reveal his strengths when he asks, "How do I pick books that kids are able to read but are not too easy or too hard?"

> This tells me that Dennis knows that quality instructional materials must provide supports **and** challenges to readers.

ACTION PLAN

Name   Dennis   **Date**   October 18

What is your current challenge in literacy instruction?

Selecting the right book for my small group reading instruction

What is/are your question/questions?

I seem to be picking books that are either too easy or too hard. How do I pick books that kids are able to read but are not too easy or too hard?

What do you know about that area, and what are you trying?

I know that I need to use my running records to help me pick the books for instruction. I am using the resource room and the levels they are currently reading at to select books but with limited success. It's more of an issue with my struggling readers.

What support do you need?

I could probably use your help in picking books, then watching me use them — is that possible?

Figure 3.2: Dennis's action plan

Dennis talks about what he knows when he says, "I need to use my running records to help me pick the books for instruction."

> This tells me he knows that running records can help with the selection of texts. I have worked with Dennis on running record analysis (Clay 2000) and I know that he is beginning to see the strength in this assessment tool.

What is Dennis trying to do in instruction? Once again, I think about what I know about Dennis's instruction from our time together and also about what he's trying in his classroom. I am seeing that he is working on planning for instruction based on his current assessment data. Dennis is using running records to determine his students' reading levels and using the school's instructional resource room to select text. But he reveals his challenge by saying he's having "limited success."

> This tells me that he can use some help selecting books using his data from the running records. My sense is that he may be selecting books based upon reading levels rather than student reading behaviors.

What do I know about Dennis's challenge to improve student learning? This question helps me think about what I know so that I can support Dennis in overcoming his challenge.

- I know that the analysis of a running record can give me a wealth of information. It provides an accuracy rate, a text level, and information about the reading behaviors the student is using.

- I know that the books are leveled in the school's instructional resource room based on the developmental stages of readers (emergent, early, and fluent). Because Dennis teaches seven year olds, his readers fit within those stages of development.

- I know that the Characteristics of Learners (Mooney 2005) can support Dennis in making the link between the reading behaviors on the running records and the features of the texts in the instructional resource room.

- I know that quality instructional texts will provide enough support for the readers to build on what they know but also enough challenges to help them with what they need to know next.

What might Dennis need to learn next? This question is not intended to provide a literal answer to me as the coach, but it's intended to be a guide in what I will be looking for when I work with Dennis. I am using my background knowledge from our work together and what Dennis has written to think about the direction we might go together. I also know that when I am working with him I might find that he has a much stronger knowledge base than I thought about his challenge, or I might also find that he needs more support than I expected. So I go in with a direction rather than a firm decision about the kind and amount of support that might be needed.

Dennis is very open with the kind of support he needs: "I could probably use your help in picking books, then watching me use them."

> It makes sense at this time to spend some time with Dennis looking at the reading groups he has formed from his running records, determining the reading behaviors he wants to develop with those students, and looking for texts that will support the development of those behaviors. I expect that he will find the Characteristics of Learners very helpful as we do this work.

I look at the notes I have about Dennis's action plan. There are a variety of strengths to build upon. Dennis understands:

- Different readers need different texts
- Texts should provide readers with supports and challenges
- Running records inform instructional text selection.

Dennis is trying to overcome his challenge. He is approximating by:

- Planning for instruction by using his reading assessments to select instructional texts (this is where he is experiencing "limited success," so I know it is a challenge).

I'm thinking about the direction Dennis and I might take in our work together. When using the assessment data from Dennis's students to select instructional texts, I'll be asking myself:

> Is Dennis using the reading level to select texts for his groups, or is he looking more carefully at the reading behaviors he would like to develop in small groups of students?

I am going to make certain that I bring the Characteristics of Learners (Mooney 2005) when we meet in the instructional resource room because I think it will help him match his students' behaviors on the assessments with the texts that support the development of those behaviors.

Gathering Information for Potential Action Plans

The coach in the school is always looking for opportunities to gather information about the strengths and the challenges of the teachers. Strengths and learning needs of teachers are revealed in many ways over the course of the school day.

Coaches listen to informal conversations with a different ear. For example, teachers sharing "something that went well" in their classrooms are making known their strengths. Comments that begin with "I'm wondering," "I'm not sure," "I'm thinking," "I hope," or "I'm frustrated by" are often disclosures of the challenges the teachers are facing with instruction and open a window to the next action plan.

Staff and grade-level meetings–meetings where teachers work and talk in small groups–are other places where coaches can learn about their colleagues. Often, people reticent about sharing in whole-staff meetings will talk openly in small groups. Charts of public notes from staff meetings can also "talk" to the coach about what colleagues know or are wondering and are another source of action plans.

The beginning of the school year is a good time for the coach to initiate informal work in teachers' classrooms. It's a time when teachers welcome an extra set of hands for gathering formative assessment data about their students. This data can begin conversations between the coach and teacher, focusing on what students can do and what they need to learn. Talking about student data opens conversations about what the teacher needs to learn as well.

The more a coach and teacher prepare together, the easier it becomes for the coach to focus on providing quality feedback to the teacher. The action plan allows the coach to determine the teacher's initial strengths and questions. Chapter 4 will explore the skills a coach needs to prepare for the job-embedded work alongside the teacher.

CHAPTER **4**

FOCUSING ON
JOB-EMBEDDED WORK

The previous chapter discussed the skills a coach needs when preparing to work with a teacher. The coach's focus for working with a teacher comes from the coach's understanding of the action plan and how to analyze it.

The most effective form of teacher support occurs on the job (Joyce and Showers 2002). Being supported on the job enables teachers not only to increase their knowledge and skill in instruction but to apply these in the classroom as well. The feedback provided to teachers by the coach about their classroom practice is a critical component of effective teaching. As mentioned previously, feedback provides the opportunity for the teachers to engage in reflection about their own practices with support from a coach. The coach needs to develop the skills of collecting information when working alongside the teachers to assist in the teachers' reflection.

A well-developed action plan provides the key to what the work alongside each teacher will look like. Through conversations with the teacher and analysis of the action plan the coach and the teacher can both see where the challenge lies. This challenge suggests where it would be best to begin working alongside the teacher.

For example, if a teacher does not have enough relevant assessment information about the learners in his or her classroom, it would be helpful for that teacher and the coach to begin to gather formative assessment information together. If a teacher is challenged with content knowledge, the coach's work begins by increasing the teacher's knowledge of content. Teachers who need to know how to use time more effectively could work with a coach on long-term, medium-term, or daily planning. And teachers whose questions deal with instruction will work with the coach in their classroom practice. The way the coach works alongside each teacher will continually change according to the teacher's current need for support.

Planning for the Job-embedded Work

Once the coach has had the opportunity to review the action plan, decisions can be made about how to best provide helpful feedback to the teacher. The teacher's questions suggest where the support should be focused.

For example, the teacher who asks, "How can I help my students select better writing topics?" would benefit from beginning to work with the coach to analyze her students' current writing topics and how they are selected.

The teacher who says, "I just don't have time to get to small group instruction" could probably use feedback about how time is being used in his classroom. A session on planning might be most helpful for that teacher.

The teacher who says, "I can't seem to select the right books for my reading groups; they are either too easy or too difficult" could find a session on instructional text selection beneficial.

And support for the teacher who says, "I want my students to talk more in small group discussion. What can I be doing to support that conversation?" will begin with the coach observing small group discussions.

As well, the amount of time spent working with each teacher depends on what support each teacher needs. Working on evaluating assessment data or planning for instruction might be best approached in a 30-minute period outside of the classroom. The time the coach spends working with the teacher during instruction might be only fifteen or twenty minutes. The time allocation will be directly related to the teacher's action plan.

Success Criteria

The action plan gives the coach a focus. The coach's success criterion is: "How might the practice look in the classroom if the teacher's question was answered?" What it looks and sounds like is what the teacher would need to know and understand.

As an example, if a teacher is interested in selecting appropriate reading material for his struggling adolescent readers, the coach will ask questions of herself to prepare for the job-embedded work:

- How would I select texts for struggling adolescent readers? What would I need to know about the students?
- What would I need to know about the texts available? What texts appeal to struggling readers?
- What have I read professionally that has helped me understand how to select texts?

The coach's answers to these questions suggest how she will work alongside the teacher and support his learning. If the coach is unsure of the answers, she will have to work to find out before she begins instructional dialogue.

Effective Note Taking

Notes taken by the coach when working with a teacher are critical to the quality of feedback that the coach provides during instructional dialogue. It's similar to a ballerina using a mirror to practice her craft. The mirror provides a reflection of her work. The coach's notes about what she sees and hears are the mirror for the teacher. The clarity of the coach's recording captures the quality of the teacher's work.

The coach's notes should be objective. The notes set out what the coach has seen and heard while working with the teacher. The coach records both teacher and student behaviors and comments and information about the resources. Judgment is reserved; the notes are simply what is seen and heard. The coach also notes her questions for later discussion. Figure 4.1 shows examples of effective note-taking strategies. This is based on the scenario that appears in Chapter 1.

It is tempting for a coach to write down everything said and heard as preparation for instructional dialogue. Usually this is more information than needed. As part of a coach's training, effective note taking is an important skill to acquire. The coach's notes begin with the teacher's questions from the action plan. Knowing exactly what the coach is looking for enables the observation to remain focused. For example, if the teacher wants support in analyzing

Jesse 1/22

AP:

Improving the comprehension of struggling readers   Questions
- Stop when it doesn't make sense?
- Meaningful substitutions (make sense and look right)?

Questions
- Is the teaching objective directly linked to the behaviors he wants his students to change?
- Amount of support—evidence of learning—too much/not enough?

Sounds in Space

What do you think this piece is going to be about?
- Rockets, aliens, space invaders—begins sharing favorite TV cartoon about space—others share cartoons about space

Look at the title of this piece. What does that make you think about?
- I think it has something to do with sounds—look at these words Boom, Roar, Zap!

Do you think this piece is fiction or nonfiction?
- I know it's fiction because look at the illustrations. It's like a comic book.
- I don't think so. If it was fiction the title might be different like Space Invaders Rise Again or something like that

(Continued discussion about fiction or nonfiction—Rich!!)

We'd better get started. Read the first page and stop if you come to any words you don't know.

Questions that focus on meaning?
Questions that focus on words?

Figure 4.1: Notes from Jesse's instruction

the effectiveness of her questioning during instruction, the coach would note each of the teacher's questions and the students' responses. If the teacher wants to focus an episode on the feedback he provides to students when they are working independently, the coach would note the feedback that the teacher provides and the students' responses to it. A column at the side of the notes is used for questions and thoughts that arise as the coach and teacher work together.

The coach objectively gathers all of the information that identifies what the teacher knows and what the teacher is beginning to know and uncovers what the teacher needs to learn next. A coach uses more than one source of information. For example, information can be gathered by listening to what teachers and students say and observing what they can do.

> A teacher was considering the effectiveness of his questioning in small group instruction. The coach wrote down the questions that the teacher asked and the responses of the students. Following the lesson, they analyzed the questions together and determined which questions were supporting the learning of students and which questions were not as effective.

Information can be gathered by looking at student work.

> A teacher was concerned about the writing development of her students. The coach looked at the student writing to see how much writing was occurring. Was it enough writing to improve the quality? As a result, the coach and teacher agreed that the quantity of students' writing had to increase before the quality of the writing would improve.

Information is gathered by talking with students.

> A teacher wanted support in knowing how her students were using their time independently while she was working with small groups. The coach walked around the classroom asking students what they were doing, why they were doing it, and what they expected to accomplish during their work time. The analysis of this data by the coach and teacher together resulted in an accountability system that assisted students to more effectively manage their time.

Information is gathered when the teacher and the coach work together.

> A teacher was struggling to select appropriate resources for her reading groups. Together the coach and teacher used the instructional resource room in the school to

locate those resources that would support different groups of students. This helped
the teacher uncover the attributes of different resources for different stages of reading
development.

Effective note taking is not limited to classroom observation. Part of the job of the coach is to think about all of the ways to support the potential learning for the teacher. Gathering data in the classroom provides just one form of support. If a teacher is learning about evaluating student assessments, a classroom observation would not be appropriate for the coach to gather relevant information to support that learning. On the other hand, if the teacher needs to learn about the impact instruction is having on student learning, the classroom is the most appropriate place to gather that information. It's the coach who learns the appropriate place to gather information to inform the dialogue.

Analyzing the Notes

Coaches are often selected because of the quality of their work as classroom teachers. They should be able to walk back into the classroom-teacher role at any time. It's very tempting for coaches to want to "fix" what they have just observed. It's often easy to see how a lesson could be done better. There is a caution here: the role of the coach is not to "fix the lesson." The role of the coach is to provide feedback to the teacher so the teacher sees how changes in his or her own practice will result in more effective instruction.

The questions asked when analyzing the data collected from working alongside the teacher are similar to the questions used when analyzing the action plan. A coach asks these questions of him- or herself to plan for a direction for instructional dialogue.

"What can the teacher do?" allows the coach to confirm the strengths from the teacher's action plan and identify new strengths. Recalling the coaching situation described previously, where the teacher and coach were selecting resources, the teacher thought she had no knowledge about selecting resources. When she and the coach looked at resources together, the coach was able to point out that indeed she knew a great deal more than she realized. The teacher had said that the students were interested in the content of the book but that the text features were a challenge to some of her students. She also mentioned that diagrams and photographs provided support. It was helpful to the teacher for the coach to point out these strengths and build upon them.

"Where is the teacher approximating?" Observing the teacher trying something new allows the coach to see where the teacher is approximating and how those approximations could be built upon. In the example in which the teacher was exploring the impact of his questioning on the learning of his students, the coach had recorded the questions that the teacher asked. In that episode, several questions had a bigger impact on the learning of the students than others. By analyzing the questions, the teacher and coach were able to decide what made those questions so successful and how the teacher could develop his questioning technique further.

"What might the teacher need to learn next?" This question provides the potential learning outcomes for instructional dialogue. When the coach gathered data on the amount of writing occurring in a classroom, she quickly found that most students were not writing daily. This data led the coach to a potential learning outcome for the teacher: to increase the frequency of student writing to daily.

These and similar questions help the coach identify learning opportunities for instructional dialogue. These learning opportunities lead teachers in the direction of learning opportunities for students as well. Analyzing the learning data also allows the coach to see the potential for both.

Planning for Instructional Dialogue

Planning for instructional dialogue is like planning for any effective instruction. The coach considers the potential learning outcomes for the teacher. She considers the resources or learning experiences that will support the teacher in reflecting on his or her teaching during the instructional dialogue. She plans by thinking about the implications that this learning will have on the teacher; what the teacher will be able to do and how the teacher will do it. Most importantly, the coach considers the evidence she expects to see in student learning that shows the impact of the change the teacher has made through the coaching experience.

There was the teacher who was interested in knowing how effectively her students were using their independent time. In this episode, the coach talked with students and asked them: "What are you doing? Why are you doing it? What do you expect to accomplish during this time?" The coach was able to quickly identify the strengths of the teacher through the quality of the student responses. The question, "Why are you doing it?" showed evidence of what the teacher was trying to do. Some students understood the expectations about reading and writing during the literacy block but just as many did not understand why they were doing what they were doing. The final question, "What do you expect to accomplish during this time?" was the most revealing. Students provided vague answers about what they were expected to accomplish. The potential learning for the teacher was pretty clear to the coach: To understand how to set expectations and ensure that students know what they are doing and productively work independently to achieve those expectations. The coach now had an idea of what to plan for instructional dialogue.

This chapter has talked about the role of the coach when working alongside the teacher, analyzing that work, and planning for instructional dialogue. Chapter 5 will focus on the instructional dialogue itself.

CHAPTER 5

CONDUCTING INSTRUCTIONAL DIALOGUE

The previous chapter considered the role of the coach in gathering information while working alongside the teacher. It explored the questions the coach asks and how those questions support the plan for instructional dialogue. It discussed how the job-embedded work can look. This chapter focuses on the role of the coach in instructional dialogue.

As noted earlier, instructional dialogue is a structured conversation about teaching and learning that provides feedback to the teacher. The measure of improvement is always student learning. It is neither an interrogation nor a therapy session. It's a dialogue between colleagues learning from each other to do their jobs better. Instructional dialogue, it was noted, is an opportunity for teachers through the mentorship and facilitation of a coach to think about their practice and ways to improve it. Figure 5.1 provides an overview of the cycle of teacher development described in this book.

The job of the coach during instructional dialogue is to:

- Lead the structured conversation
- Listen carefully for what the teacher already knows and what the teacher can learn next
- Know when to ask questions and when to provide answers and strategies for implementation
- Support the teacher in making a direct link between his or her learning and the learning of the students.

In this chapter we examine instructional dialogue and the implications for the work of the coach.

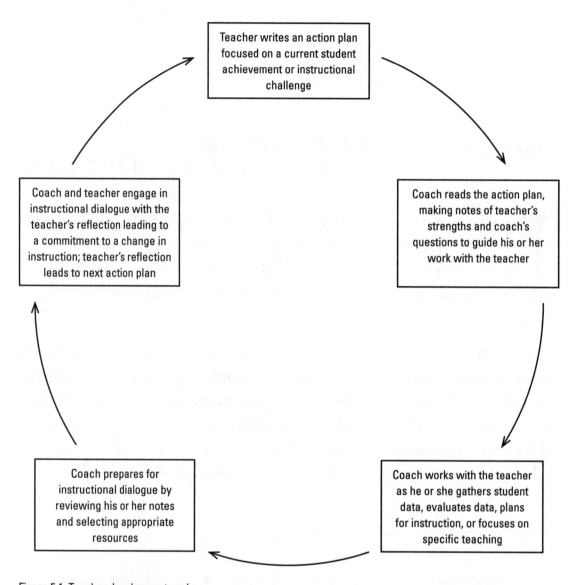

Figure 5.1: Teacher development cycle

A Structured Conversation

Chapter 2 described the roles and responsibilities of the teacher and the coach. Leading the "structured conversation" is one of these responsibilities. A regular time is established for instructional dialogue. This means that the teacher and the coach have a scheduled and uninterrupted opportunity for discussion and feedback. Schools arrange for this time in many different ways. Some schools provide classroom coverage immediately following the work alongside the teacher. Other schools see the dialogue as part of the teacher's planning time one day per week or every other week. Regardless of how it is scheduled, it's the regularity of feedback that is important.

Instructional dialogue is systematic and focused. Because it is preceded by the teacher's action plan and job-embedded work with the teacher and the coach, both participants can have certain expectations. It will be focused on the current challenge the teacher is experiencing and has identified as a focus for coaching. It will be supported by the data the coach has collected while working with the teacher. It results in the teacher making a commitment to change in instruction. That change is expected to increase student achievement.

Listening and Questioning Effectively

One of the most important skills a coach can develop is learning how to listen. Listening effectively is a highly developed skill. Listening allows the coach to identify an entry point to the teacher's learning. When given time to talk about his or her teaching, the teacher usually shares a specific challenge in the first few minutes of the conversation. A skilled listener can quickly confirm strengths and uncover these challenges if a teacher is unable to.

The coach can begin the dialogue in a number of ways to get the conversation started. For example, a teacher who is gathering formative assessment data might be invited to talk about "how it went" or "what you learned about your students." A teacher who is exploring questioning in small group instruction might be asked, "What were some of the things you heard your kids say today?" The teacher selecting resources for his instruction might be asked to share what he's thinking about now, since he and the coach worked together to select literacy resources. These initial questions are designed to be open ended enough to encourage conversation. The purpose is to make the beginning of the dialogue risk free; an opportunity for a teacher to reflect on the challenge being experienced and what is needed to overcome it.

Once the teacher begins to talk, the coach listens carefully. For many coaches, this is challenging. Some coaches might feel that just listening means that they are not doing their job. On the contrary, appropriate, meaningful feedback means coaches have to listen actively for the right time to provide that feedback.

Questions are an integral part of instructional dialogue. It's the coach's ability to listen that leads to the appropriate questions. The questions the coach asks during instructional dialogue come from what the teacher says. The questions aren't scripted; they are based upon the direction the coach has determined for the dialogue and the responses of the teacher. They are not the "guess what's in my head" kind of questions, but are those that uncover the fundamental beliefs teachers have and challenge them to extend their thinking. Note the following exchange between Alex, a teacher seeking feedback about her students' engagement in independent work, and myself.

Listening and Questioning in Action

Marilyn: How did you feel about your students' engagement during independent work time today?

This question confirms the teacher's action plan and provides time for her to talk.

Alex: Not much differently than I feel any day. I can tell you right now the names of the students who are working hard and seem involved in their work. And I can tell you the names of the students who look like they are wasting their time and mine too!

What the teacher says about knowing who was engaged and who was not engaged leads to my next question.

Marilyn: Let's talk about some of those kids who are engaged and some you feel aren't engaged. If we compare our observations, maybe we can come to some conclusions.

Alex: That's easy. (She begins by talking about the students who are not engaged. I suggest a shift in focus in the conversation.)

I suggest this shift in focus because I want Alex to begin with her students' strengths. She needs to see that she has contributed to what her students are doing well.

Marilyn:	Let's start by talking about the students who are engaged first.

Alex:	That's easy, too. (Alex talks about the students who are consistently engaged in their independent work. She names some of the same students that I have interviewed.)

Stopping the conversation and asking the teacher to analyze what is working in her classroom helps her focus on his learners' strengths. It also leads to the establishment of expectations for all students based upon the behaviors of some students.

Marilyn:	I came to the same conclusion about some of those same students. Let me share with you what I asked them and what they said. That might help us come up with some behaviors we want all of your students to have. I asked the students three questions: "What are you doing? Why are you doing it?" and "What do you expect to accomplish today?"

Let's start with Tanisha. She was reading independently when I interviewed her. I asked her what she was doing and she said, "Reading *Winn Dixie*" (DiCamillo 2000). I asked her why she was reading this book. She replied, "I like books about girls my age and dogs. My teacher told us about this book. In fact, he read some of it aloud to us and I thought I'd like it. I just started it but already I like it. I was right."

I asked her one more question: "What do you expect to accomplish today in reading?" She answered, "I want to read until I find out if the girl's dad lets her keep Winn Dixie. Did you know this dog was named for a grocery store?" She laughed.

I share a few more examples of students engaged in reading. The students make similar comments.

Marilyn:	What are you thinking now?

Alex:	Can I clone those kids? That's just how I would like all my students to talk about their independent reading.

Marilyn:	I couldn't agree with you more. Let's figure out what they were doing. What were some of the commonalities? For instance, what expectations had they set for themselves about their reading?
Alex:	Well, they all knew that they had to find a book that was interesting to them.
Marilyn:	So that's one thing we have to determine. Are the disengaged kids interested in their independent reading books?
Alex:	Not only interested, but are they able to read them and make meaning.
Marilyn:	Why don't you take a minute and write down what you are thinking.

I remind Alex to take a few notes so that she has something to refer back to after our dialogue is finished. I also use her notes as an assessment sample—an opportunity to confirm that she understands what I think she understands.

Alex takes a few notes. She writes, "Students must be interested in their books and be able to make meaning from them."

Marilyn:	What else were those students doing? Remember when I asked Tanisha what she expected to accomplish today? She said, "I want to read until I find out if the girl's dad lets her keep Winn Dixie. Did you know this dog was named for a grocery store?"
Alex:	She was setting a goal. So what I want my students to think about is what they want to accomplish as readers. Not how many pages they'll read per day, which is what I'm having them do now. That takes very little thinking. Tanisha was thinking about what she wanted to find out as she was making her way through the beginning of *Because of Winn Dixie.*
Marilyn:	This is what I hear you saying. By listening to what those kids said, you have come up with three expectations for all of your students: books that interest them; books they can read with understanding; and being able to determine what they want to accomplish as a reader to set a goal for their independent reading time. Am I right?
Alex:	Yes, but I think I've told them that a bunch of times.

This is an indication to me that Alex isn't sure what to do next even if she has a clear idea of what she wants the students to do. She has already exhausted all of her ideas. I think she knows more than she thinks she knows, so my task is to provide more support. I do that by making the next question more specific.

Marilyn:	So let's look at the difference between telling students what to do and setting expectations for how they will do it. What might that look and sound like? What would your role be, and what would your students' role be?
Alex:	I guess my role is determining if the book they are reading is engaging and if they can read it with meaning.
Marilyn:	Would you expect that to always be your role?
Alex:	Well, it's probably always going to be my role to make sure it's happening, but I would sure like it if they knew how to do those things themselves.
Marilyn:	I agree. I guess that's why we call it independent reading, because ultimately we want them doing this independently.
Alex:	So maybe that's what I work on this week. I could be determining who is reading a book that interests them and that they can read with meaning.
Marilyn:	How will you do that?

I am aware of the importance of Alex having a strategy for putting into practice what we are talking about immediately. The remainder of the dialogue is spent moving from talk to action by planning how Alex will use her time to implement this new strategy.

Alex:	I guess I'll start with the students that I know aren't in a book that's working and I'll try to figure out why. I can listen to them read a little bit and talk to them about why I pick certain books.
Marilyn:	Let's think about your time. What will you need to do with individuals and what might you be doing with small groups or the whole group?

I want Alex to see that she can use her time effectively by meeting with small groups and the whole group to reach his outcomes.

Alex: I'll need to meet with some of the students individually who don't have a book that's working, but I bet I could talk with some in small groups. I could also talk with the whole group about why I choose books to read and how I know if they are working for me.

Marilyn: Who else could share some experiences in book selection?

> I'm reminding Alex that she knows another way to save instructional time. She often has students provide demonstrations.

Alex: Oh—my kids who are engaged. I could ask them the same questions you asked them, but do it in front of the whole group.

Marilyn: And don't forget why Tanisha decided to read *Winn Dixie*.

Alex: Yes! She wanted to read it after she heard me reading a portion to the class. I could do that with a lot of high-interest books.

Marilyn: It sounds like you have some great ideas. Let's look at how we could plan for them over the next week—what you'll do with the whole group and with individuals.

We spend the next ten minutes planning for the week and setting out the support she might need. Then I conclude this part of the dialogue.

> I bring the dialogue to closure by summarizing what has been learned, why it has been learned, and the commitment to change in practice. My goal is that Alex will implement this new learning.

Marilyn: So let's think about the steps we went through today and why. First we talked about what your students are doing who are really engaged. What did that enable us to do?

Alex: We could figure out what we wanted all students to do.

Marilyn: Yes, we basically set expectations for independent reading. What else did we do?

Alex: We determined how to communicate those expectations to the students and planned for it.

Marilyn:	Let's jot those two steps down. They seem pretty simple, and I bet we could apply them to other areas of your room once we work through independent reading.

Alex and I are very interested in monitoring the result of this action plan, so I say to her: "Let's jot those two steps down on your next action plan."

We both knew that a higher level of engagement from her students would have a big impact on her ability to meet with small groups and individuals. Alex spent the next two weeks setting expectations and providing demonstrations for the whole group. At the same time she was collecting data about the readers who were not engaged in independent reading. Eventually, all but three of her students were able to remain engaged in independent reading. Alex planned daily for monitoring those three students to increase their levels of engagement.

An additional benefit of her work was the increased fluency in reading of her students. Because they were reading more often and for longer periods of time, they were able to read more fluently, which also improved their comprehension.

When to Listen; When to Question; When to Tell

Previously, feedback was defined as the opportunity for teachers to reflect on their own practices with support from a colleague. Teachers are provided with the appropriate amount of support they need for learning. Learning occurs in different ways for different individuals. This chapter has discussed the importance of the coach's skill in knowing how to listen. It has also emphasized the need for the coach to know when to ask questions appropriate to the level of the teacher's current knowledge. It's just as important for the coach to know when to let the teacher work through an issue him- or herself; in other instances simply to tell. The effective coach knows when to listen, when to ask, and when to tell.

For instance, a teacher had pulled together a reading group and requested that the coach observe how well she had reached her teaching objective. In the lesson, her students sailed right through the reading with no difficulty whatsoever. The teacher turned to the coach and said, "My problem isn't with the teaching objective, it's with the selection of text. That's what I need to focus on." Here, all the teacher required was listening to herself and acting on her intuition.

Teachers often learn by talking through and responding to the questions that are posed to them. A teacher was concerned that his students were not focused on meaning when they were reading. The coach noted each of the teacher's questions asked during a reading group and found that they were mostly questions about reading accurately. By re-reading the teacher's questions and asking if they were focused on meaning or words, the coach allowed the teacher to see that he was more focused on his students getting the words right than on them making sense of the book. The teacher was able to restructure his questions to be more meaningful. Here, the coach was able to allow the teacher to reflect by noting the questions the teacher asked.

In other situations, a teacher comes close to knowing but needs someone to tell. In this instance, a teacher had come to the realization during a dialogue that spellers had to be able to ask themselves if the word "looked right" in order to proofread their writing for spelling. When the coach asked how this might look in her classroom, the teacher said she had few ideas. Here, the coach simply gave the teacher some strategies to try with her students.

Improvement in Student Learning

Teachers' commitment to change in instruction occurs when they see themselves putting into practice what they have learned. Teachers begin to understand something new and see it as something they can add to what they do already. The test is leaving a dialogue with the confidence that they can put their new learning into place immediately. An effective coach should be able to tell when a teacher's learning occurs. What does it sound like when the teacher gets it? What support will the teacher need to put it into practice?

Coaches who understand that the test of effective teaching is increased student achievement use student data as the basis for dialogue. Student data uncovers the gap between what teachers know and what they need to know to ensure student growth.

In an earlier example, there was a teacher who was seeing little growth in her students' writing. The coach collected information in the classroom on both the quantity and quality of writing. She found that few students were writing daily. Bringing that student data to the dialogue and sharing it with the teacher allowed them to think together about strategies and set expectations with students about daily writing.

In another example, a teacher was concerned by the lack of growth in his least-proficient readers. The coach administered a running record (Clay 2000) to some of his less-proficient students. These running records were useful data in the instructional dialogue and provided information to both coach and teacher for possible next steps.

Student data helps uncover a teacher's concern and provides content and support regarding how this might be more effective for students' learning during the dialogue. A skilled coach supports the teacher in knowing what data to collect from students and how to recognize success in student learning.

The teacher who wished to ensure that writing was occurring daily developed clear expectations with her students. She then monitored the daily writing with a monitoring sheet. Each student was asked at the beginning of the writing period what part of the writing process he or she would be working on that day. During the last ten minutes of the writing period the teacher monitored her students' progress. The coach and teacher reviewed this monitoring sheet over the next two weeks and found that most students were having problems with topic selection. Further work on topics for writing was the beginning of improving the quality of student writing.

The teacher who lacked progress with his less-proficient readers made a commitment to learn more about the analysis of running records. He administered running records over the following week on these students and worked with the coach on this analysis. He was then able to establish more accurate teaching objectives for this group of students, which led to growth in their learning.

Student data becomes the evidence that a change in the teacher's instruction has had an impact. Deciding what is expected in students' learning allows the teacher to take a small enough step to experience success quickly. Effective coaches know what realistic expectations will look like and what data needs to be collected to show the evidence of growth.

Colleagues Learning to Do Their Jobs Better

The purpose of coaching is to support teachers as they extend and refine their knowledge and application of effective instruction. As a result, student learning increases. Without coaching, teachers are expected to do this alone. The skill of the coach lies in developing a relationship of trust and confidence that enables work with the teacher to be collaborative. It doesn't work if teachers believe that coaching is something that is being done **to** them.

"We" is important for coaches. Making a commitment to change is much easier when teachers feel as if they are doing it with someone who is a supportive colleague. Note the two conversations below between coach and teacher. Ask yourself which conversation feels more inclusive.

Coach:	I want you to see this running record I took on one of your less-proficient students. It can really tell you what their challenges are. (The coach reads through the running record.) So, what do you think you should do next?
Teacher:	Learn about running records, I guess.
Coach:	If you take running records on some of your students next week, I can help you learn to analyze them.

In this example the coach is telling the teacher what to do. The message is: I'll tell you what to do because I know and then I'll check to see if you have done it.

The following conversation is on the same topic.

Coach:	I was thinking about the challenge you are facing with your struggling readers and thought about an assessment tool I've used to help get to the bottom of the challenges these readers are facing. I took a couple of running records on your kids and wanted to share what I found to see if it will help us. (The coach talks aloud through the analysis of the running record and describes what she saw the student doing as a developing reader.) What are you thinking?
Teacher:	I didn't really know they weren't making sense of what they were reading until I saw what you did.

Coach:	I'm thinking that if we took some more running records over the next week on the other kids in that group, then we could work together to analyze them. Are you comfortable taking them?
Teacher:	I can take them, but I'm not comfortable with what you just did.
Coach:	I can understand that. It took me awhile to remember how to analyze too, but if we can do it together it should be quick and easy.

Similar outcomes were established in these two conversations. The difference is in the style of support. In both, the teacher committed to taking running records on his less-proficient students, and the running record would be analyzed. The latter example suggests colleagues working together. Coaches consider that their role is to help teachers solve problems that they are unable to solve alone. Effective coaches work in collaboration with the teachers.

Chapters 3, 4, and 5 have examined the role of the coach in planning for instructional dialogue. Chapter 6 shows a teacher and coach putting it all together.

CHAPTER 6   PUTTING IT ALL TOGETHER: JAN AND MARILYN

Jan is a multi-age first- and second-grade teacher in a school in the sixth-largest urban school district in Colorado. Seventy-six percent of the school's population receives a free or reduced-price lunch. The school's ethnicity is 52 percent Hispanic, 28 percent black, 18 percent white, 1 percent Asian, and 1 percent American Indian. More than half of the school's students are new learners of English. This chapter analyzes the process of instructional dialogue in action with Jan, where I had the role of coach. The DVD accompanying this book shows the actual instructional dialogue.

Jan's Action Plan and Marilyn's Note Taking

Jan has been working on understanding revision in the writing process. I analyze Jan's action plan (Figure 6.1), beginning with her strengths:

- She uses the analysis of her students' writing to identify her own challenge with instruction. ("My students are good writers, but when I look at their writing, I see that they go back and add to the end, not go back and add in the words where they would make sense. They will answer the question orally but then add it to the end.")
- She knows the purpose of revision is to make the writing clear for the reader. ("How can I get them to see that the revision is to help the reader?" "Kids need to know authors have a need to convey ideas that involve playing with words, testing them for clarity; wrestling with them to make meaning to the reader.").

I make a note to confirm that what Jan knows matches what she is doing during instruction. Jan has set out the purpose of revision in her action plan, but does she revise with the reader in mind when she is teaching?

ACTION PLAN

Name   *Jan*   **Date**   *April 2*

What is your current challenge in literacy instruction?

Revision in writing—My students are good writers, but when I look at their writing, I see that they go back and add to the end, not go back and add in the words where they would make sense. They will answer the question orally but then add it to the end.

What is/are your question/questions?

How can I get them to see that the revision is to help the reader?
In my demonstrations, am I thinking aloud enough?
Am I making it understood that I need to make my writing as clear as possible?

What do you know about that area, and what are you trying?

I know that a writer uses revision to effectively improve communication. Kids need to know authors have a need to convey ideas that involve playing with words, testing them for clarity; wrestling with them to make meaning to the reader.
I've been trying to focus my demonstrations on revising.

What support do you need?

I have been trying to demonstrate what a writer does to clarify meaning. I'd like you to watch my demonstration to see if I'm doing that. I'd like to see if you can tell what the kids are thinking by what they're saying.

Figure 6.1: Jan's action plan

I think about what Jan is trying to do, which is an indication that she is approximating or coming to know something. I consider what she might need to learn next. Her action plan implies that she understands why writers revise, but I see that her challenge is supporting her students to not only understand why writers revise but how they revise as well. Jan says in her action plan: "I've been trying to focus my demonstrations on revising." "I have been trying to demonstrate what a writer does to clarify meaning." Watching her instruction will allow me, her coach, to see if she is demonstrating the decisions that writers have to make when they revise. I will look to see if her revisions will make the product clearer for the reader, but I also wonder if Jan is thinking about the process the writer has to understand to get to that product.

Jan has been specific in the support she desires. She says, "I have been trying to demonstrate what a writer does to clarify meaning. I'd like you to watch my demonstration to see if I'm doing that." It's obvious that she is looking for feedback about her writing instruction.

My work with Jan will be an observation of her demonstrating writing to her whole group of students. She seeks feedback from me about how she revises her writing in front of the students. I will be watching for a demonstration of the decisions that writers make when they revise–why to revise, where revisions are needed, and how to revise. I know the purpose of a quality demonstration is to think aloud about how writers write. Jan asks if she is "thinking aloud enough." I also am going to be focused on what she is thinking aloud about.

Figure 6.2 sets out the structure of my note taking in Jan's classroom. At the top of the page, I've written Jan's questions to remind me of what I'm looking for. Beneath the questions are two columns. In this observation, I will use the first column to record what either Jan or the students say or do. The second column is for my reflections and questions.

Working with Jan on the Job

This section illustrates how I worked with Jan as her coach. Jan arranged for me to be in her classroom to see a writing demonstration. I have already seen her action plan (Figure 6.1) and have some ideas about what she was looking for. My note-taking page (Figure 6.2) has her ques-

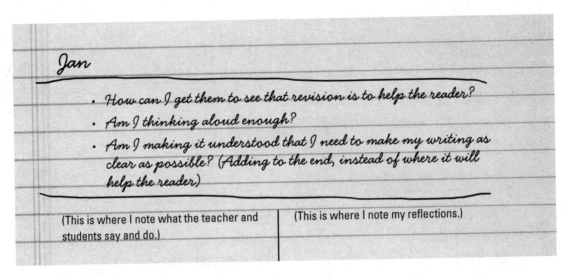

Figure 6.2: Structure for note taking

tions at the top to help me focus on what I will be observing. The bottom of my note page is divided for note taking; I will record what I observe in the first column and I will use the second column to note my thoughts or questions.

Jan is ready to begin her writing demonstration on revision for her students as I enter her classroom. The students are seated on the floor, and a chart tablet is in front of them. Jan begins to demonstrate writing for her students. Her actions confirm for me some of her strengths. She notes the quality and clarity of her students' writing. She says that the writing created a picture in her mind, which is important for a reader. The children agree. Her comments confirm what I anticipated; she had selected the learning objective for this teaching because of what she saw her students doing. I make a note of that information (see Figure 6.3).

Jan continues to talk aloud about her writing and the person her piece of writing was for. She is writing about an experience she had had. The writing will be for her neighbor, Sarah. Jan mentions thinking about her writing while driving to school. She has decided that she isn't really happy with it. She knows it is a great story, but she doesn't know if it will give Sarah a "picture in her head." Once again, Jan is confirming what I thought: her understanding of the

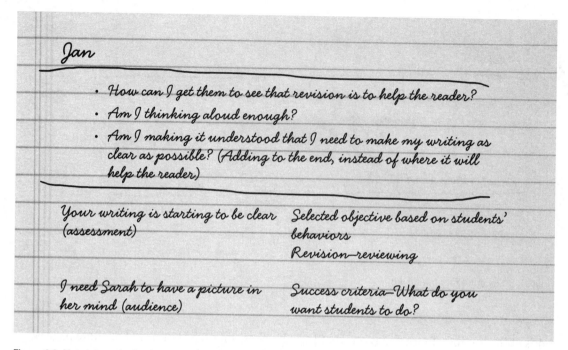

Figure 6.3: Notes from the beginning of Jan's writing demonstration

importance of the audience to the writer is helping her make certain that the meaning will be clear to the reader. I jot that down because I want to be able to share with Jan evidence about what she knows about revision.

I wonder if she has thought about how she wants her students to revise. Her action plan noted that revisions need to make writing clear. What does this mean to her students? What decisions will they be making as writers? I note my questions on my note-taking page.

Jan continues to talk about how she revises her writing with her students. She talks about re-reading the story to herself twice to make sure she hasn't missed anything. I remember the question she asked in her action plan, "Am I thinking aloud enough?" I wonder again, is her question about "thinking aloud enough" or is her question really, "What am I thinking aloud about?" I make another note: "What will Sarah need to know?" I'm wondering if that kind of thinking aloud would help Jan's students begin to think more like writers.

Jan begins to read her writing and finds a place where she has forgotten a word. She reads on to another place where she feels the writing is not clear enough. She says, "I want to add it right here." I make a note of her revision and also write: "Where should I put this revision?"–a question that will show more than what the writer does. It will show how the writer thinks. I am thinking again about the decisions a writer makes while revising.

Jan is doing a good job of explaining why writers revise, but I am not sure that her students understand it. I write two notes to myself: "Why do we revise? How do we revise?" My notes appear in Figure 6.4.

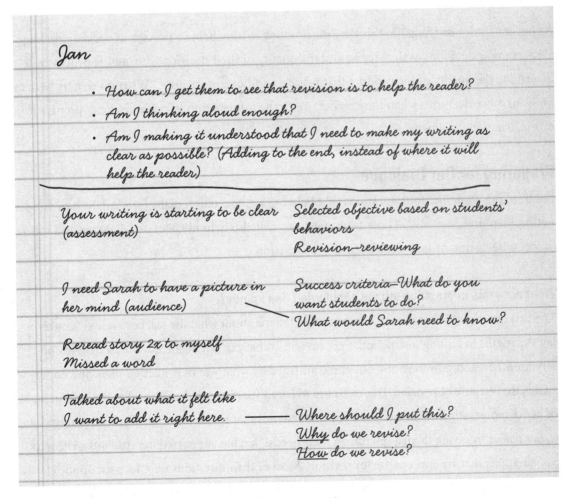

Figure 6.4: Notes focusing on revision from Jan's writing demonstration

Jan re-reads her piece again. She likes the revisions she has made and feels that they will help Sarah get a better picture of what happened, she explains. She asks the class if they have any "I wonder" questions. I note how the children question. It is obvious that she has had them focus their questions on the meaning of the piece. They ask:

- I wonder: did Mr. Lasater have gloves on too?
- I wonder: What color was the baby bird?

Jan talks about how she will answer these questions by further revising the piece. I add more to my notes (Figure 6.5).

As Jan concludes revising, I'm thinking more about writing being a process of decision making. Writers make decisions as they revise and the quality of their decisions during the process will determine the quality of the product that results. I add one more note: "What do writers have to know to make decisions when they revise?" With the information in my notes I can prepare for our instructional dialogue.

Preparing for Our Dialogue

I'm thinking about the four questions that help me analyze action plans (see "Analysis of an Action Plan" in Chapter 3). Those four questions will also help me plan our dialogue and reflect on my observation of Jan's demonstration of revision.

What does this information tell me about what Jan knows?

The first question, "What does this information tell me about what the teacher knows?" concerns Jan's strengths in writing instruction. I ask myself: "What can Jan do already?" Based on my observation, her strengths were obvious and confirmed by what was in her action plan. She understands the purpose of revision. Her reference to Sarah (her intended audience) at the beginning of her demonstration confirmed that. She understands that revision is to make the meaning clear to her reader by giving them a "picture in their heads." Jan has supported her students in how to ask questions that are appropriate for revision. Most of their questions were focused on the clarity

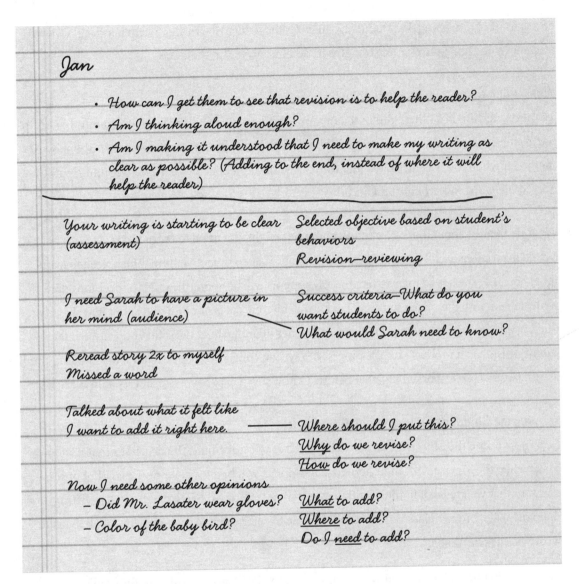

Jan

- How can I get them to see that revision is to help the reader?
- Am I thinking aloud enough?
- Am I making it understood that I need to make my writing as clear as possible? (Adding to the end, instead of where it will help the reader)

Your writing is starting to be clear (assessment)

Selected objective based on student's behaviors
Revision—reviewing

I need Sarah to have a picture in her mind (audience)

Success criteria—What do you want students to do?
What would Sarah need to know?

Reread story 2x to myself
Missed a word

Talked about what it felt like
I want to add it right here.

Where should I put this?
Why do we revise?
How do we revise?

Now I need some other opinions
  – Did Mr. Lasater wear gloves?
  – Color of the baby bird?

What to add?
Where to add?
Do I need to add?

Figure 6.5: Noting students' questions and Jan's response

or details of her meaning. Jan frequently analyzes the students' writing to help her decide what to teach next. She has a number of strengths to build upon in this dialogue.

What is Jan trying to do in instruction?

My next question is: "Where did I see Jan approximate a new skill?" There were a number of opportunities. Jan talked with the students about the need to read their pieces twice. She showed them that when she was missing some words, she said to herself: "That didn't sound right. I missed the word. Where should I add this?"

What do I know about Jan's challenge and what might she need to learn next?

My final questions are, "What do I know about Jan's challenge and what might Jan need to learn next?" Because she has so many strengths, my support will be about the kinds of decisions that writers make with the reader in mind. Jan knows this, but she is not thinking about it as she is conducting this writing demonstration. I would like her to understand the difference between the result of revision as a product and the process of revision concerned with what the writer has to think about. Jan and I have worked together before. I know this will probably be an easy shift for her.

Framing the Objective for Instructional Dialogue

I can now frame the objective for our dialogue. It is to understand the decisions that writers make when they revise with their audience in mind. I will bring a copy of the writing process diagram that we are both familiar with to the dialogue. Jan will bring her students' writing. Our dialogue will be in her classroom. We will be able to refer to her actual revision work that she wrote on the chart tablet.

The following instructional dialogue is shown on the DVD accompanying this book.

Jan's Instructional Dialogue

Because of my experiences coaching Jan, I know that she will have already reflected on her teaching experience and her action plan. I know that she will have something to say, so I ask an open question: "What did you think?"

Jan shares the formative data she has collected about her students' writing. She says that their revisions show her two things. They are either not adding anything to revise or adding all of their revisions to the end of their writing. This statement and the stack of student writing on the table show me that she uses student work to select the focus for her instruction. She continues to reflect:

Jan: I'm hoping I've made it clear enough to my students that the revision needs to be in the story.

> As a coach, I listen for phrases like "I'm hoping...," or "I'm wondering...," or "I'm not sure." These phrases often occur early in the dialogue and are an indication that the teacher does not have the confidence or evidence that the students learned from the instruction.

Jan makes an important comment that confirms what she has written in her action plan.

Jan: My students don't understand that it's the reader that has to have [the question] answered rather than the person you are reading it to.

> I write down what she has said because I will be able to use her statement later in the dialogue. I want Jan to talk about the expectations she has for her writers.

Marilyn: Talk about what you would like your students to be able to do in the next three weeks, when they have a better understanding of revision.

> I ask Jan this question to determine if she is thinking about the decisions that writers make (the process) or if she is focused on the product (the end result).

Jan talks about wanting her students to add descriptive words and to add action. I remind her that what she has described is the product–what the writing will look like.

> I ask a more specific question. I want her to think about what writers do.

Marilyn: What will the writer have to do to make that happen?

Jan talks about visualizing, re-living the event, and picturing what happened. I realize that I need to provide more support by asking some focused questions.

> I know from experience that teachers can make connections to their students' learning when they think about themselves as readers and writers, so I ask her to think about herself as a writer.

Marilyn: When you revise as a writer, what are you thinking?

Jan: I'm thinking does it make sense, does it sound right to me, is it clear?

> I need to dig a bit deeper by going back to her demonstration. I'm pretty sure she'll begin to think about who she is writing for.

Marilyn: Who were you writing that piece for today?

Jan: Oh, I'm also thinking what Sarah understands.

> I can see her making a connection. She continues and I listen.

Jan: Okay. I'm thinking about what my audience understands and what will make it clear to them. So that's the **why** behind the product. I need to talk about the audience a lot more. Sarah would need to know these things. Or if we write about the butterfly that hatched in our classroom, we need to make it clear to someone who was absent when it happened, like Devon.

> I come back to the statement I have recorded in my notes to confirm that she is now seeing how to apply what she has already talked about.

Marilyn: You said earlier that the reader needs to have the question answered, not the person you're reading it to. So the writer is always thinking about what to do to make it clear to the reader.

> Jan begins to write down what she's thinking on an instructional dialogue sheet to keep a record of her thinking. I know the importance of giving time for the teacher to take some notes. These notes are not only helpful for the teacher following the dialogue, but they also give me a window into the learning that is occurring.

Marilyn: What did you write?

Her written responses help me decide where to go next in the dialogue. Do I need to provide more support, or can we continue to move on?

Jan: (reads her bulleted notes) Who will be reading this? Keep the audience in mind. What will they have to know to make a picture in their head?

I am confident that Jan is clear about the purpose of revision and how that will sound in her demonstration. I also know that Jan is willing to continue our conversation.

Marilyn: Let's go back to the idea of product and process. If we're developing the writer, which is what I know you are interested in doing, what is going on inside the writer's head when they're revising?

Jan: They're thinking about who they are revising for and if it's clear to their audience. They might be thinking about the vocabulary they'd use.

I realize that the question I asked was too broad. I narrow it by going back to Jan as a writer herself. Jan makes great connections when she thinks about her own writing.

Marilyn: What would you be saying inside your head when you've written a parent letter and you're re-reading it?

Jan: What do my parents need to know? What do I want them to remember after they have read it? Have I made it clear?

This is exactly what I expected to hear. I know that we can make another direct link between Jan as a writer and what she will expect her students to understand.

Marilyn: Listen to what you said. (I repeat her questions) What are all of those?

Jan: Those are questions you need to ask yourself. Okay. . .

The light goes on again, and I know she understands that writers need to ask questions of themselves as they write.

Marilyn: What do you want your kids doing?

Jan: Asking questions as they are writing! Oh, geez!

Jan returns to her notes and adds more to what she has already written.

Jan: I think what my students think is, I'm going to ask questions after I'm done writing instead of **when** I'm writing.

I go back to Jan's action plan to refer to a question she asked. I am sure that she will be able to answer her own question now.

Marilyn: So when you think about your demonstrations, one of the questions you asked was, "In my demonstrations, am I thinking aloud enough?" What should you be thinking aloud about?

Jan: The questions. I should be asking myself questions as we go.

Marilyn: So what might that sound like?

This is where we will begin taking the new learning and determining what it will look like in practice. I expect that Jan will have no problem with this, but I want to make sure.

Jan goes back to the demonstration she did earlier and articulates the kinds of questions that will support her writers.

I now see that Jan understands why writers revise and what they need to ask themselves. The last bit I want to talk about with Jan are the decisions that writers make when they are revising. I'm thinking that this conversation will require more support from me.

Marilyn: That takes care of what it needs to sound like in their heads and what it needs to sound like out of your mouth. Let's take it one step further and think about the placement of your revisions. If we're going back to writers as questioners of themselves as they write, how does that impact the revision placement?

Jan: Is it more in the composing part? Do I go back and ask myself questions while I'm composing?

Marilyn: You might be. But when do you figure out as a writer that you've left something out?

Jan: After you've re-read.

Marilyn: So at that point in time, what are you saying to yourself?

Jan: What did I forget? What does my audience still need to know?

Marilyn: That's what you're going to put in your piece of writing, but you still have one more question before you do that.

Part of the skill in coaching is knowing when to continue to ask questions of the teacher and when to stop asking questions and tell the teacher what she needs to know. I realize that asking more questions may result in frustration on Jan's part. She's already done a lot of thinking during this dialogue. So I decide to tell her and work from there.

Marilyn: The question the writer needs to ask is: "Where will I put this revision?"

In the statement below, I demonstrate for Jan what it would sound like when a writer thinks about where to put the revisions.

Marilyn: "Where does it need to go to make the most sense to my reader? This is what's missing. Gosh, should I put it at the end? No, that wouldn't make sense!" So that's another thing we need to ask.

Jan: Not only what will we revise but where will we put it.

I'm ready to bring closure to this dialogue. I'm keeping track of how long we have been working together. I know that Jan has learned enough to make some productive changes in her demonstrations.

Marilyn: Tell me what you're thinking now about your understanding of revision.

Jan: I need to get away from the product and think about the process a lot more and bring that forward to the kids. Writers have to ask questions the whole time so their audience understands what they're writing.

Marilyn: Great! Write that down.

I want to leave Jan with a strategy for revision that I don't think she's tried but which will support what she's learned today. Jan's students are very engaged in their independent work. So I share a strategy for using slips of paper for students to record questions during small group writing conferences. I can already visualize her students in these small group writing conferences.

Marilyn: I want the students taking those questions back to their seats. Why would I want them to do that?

Jan: They're jotting down questions other writers ask. The writer takes the questions away. If I'm writing it for someone to read, those are the questions the reader might have. I'm in the audience position.

Marilyn: What else do the writers have to do when they take those questions back to their seats?

Jan: Think about where they're going to place them.

Marilyn: Yes, and think about the question one of your kids asked about the egg falling out of the nest. What decision did you make as a writer?

Jan: It wasn't important to my story. Oh. . .You want a writer to say, "I don't have to put that in." I wondered about that.

Marilyn: Being a good writer means being able to make decisions about where things go and how I'm going to do it.

Jan: Oh. . .

Marilyn: What will that look like when you are demonstrating?

Jan easily talks about how she will jot down the questions her students ask one day and return to them the next day to model her decision-making process about which revisions are important to her audience and where they will go.

Marilyn: Yep–you're modeling how a writer who is revising thinks.

The impact of the change in Jan's writing demonstrations is immediate with some of her students. Some students informally have conferences with their peers for revision and use scraps of paper to write their questions on. Jan sees a marked difference in her small group conferences. Some of these students who have taken on the new understanding of revision demonstrate the same kind of questioning she has used with her own writing. Jan is pleased with the enthusiasm and independence of her young writers. More importantly, she is delighted with the impact on the quality of their writing.

Listening, asking, telling–each is part of the collegial relationship that develops between the coach and teacher. It's not only the teacher who has learned and committed to trying something with her students. When working with Jan, I learned as well. Coaches learn about their colleagues and they learn from confirming hunches. They also learn that coaching is a partnership to which both teacher and coach contribute. The partnership is about bringing out the best in both; becoming a more effective teacher and becoming a more effective coach. And both contribute to improving the achievement of every student. Chapter 7 suggests strategies toward implementing this type of successful literacy coaching school wide.

PART 3:
Ensuring that the Process of Instructional Dialogue Works

CHAPTER 7   SETTING THE STAGE FOR SUCCESSFUL LITERACY COACHING

This book attempts to explain the process coaches need to understand to be successful in their work with teachers. It discusses the importance of the development of a collegial relationship between the coach and the teacher. It looks at the action plan as a tool for both teacher and coach in uncovering an instructional challenge and acting upon it and explores the skills coaches need to analyze action plans and plan for the job-embedded support of the teacher. This book also investigates the expertise a coach needs to facilitate instructional dialogue. Finally, as a support, a DVD has been provided to demonstrate the process of instructional dialogue in action.

Setting the Stage for Success

When a teacher and coach have developed a supportive coaching relationship, the likelihood of success is quite high. But a school-wide coaching initiative requires work to be done prior to beginning the coaching experience. There is a need for a school to agree about how coaching will be implemented as a process for professional development. These agreements help clarify for all individuals how professional development with coaching will work. The process should be transparent. There can be no hidden agendas. Everyone should be aware of the part they play and the responsibility they have toward increasing student achievement. This chapter describes a school process for developing those agreements.

Being Transparent

Teachers who are resistant to change often feel that way because of their prior experiences with the way changes have been implemented. They become "gun shy." When it is announced that, "We are going to learn to do guided reading in this school," teachers often feel they receive minimal support to implement this change. When they are told, "We're going to have an inservice on guided reading, and then we'll follow that up with a book study," they often feel that the only support that is available is a formula for complying with the change. When they hear that, "This is how you 'do' guided reading," they are simply exposed to a procedure or practice that they are expected to implement in their classroom without support.

Teachers who feel a responsibility toward their students find uncertainty difficult. They cannot wait. They feel they have to do what they know is best for their students. They expect any new change will go away or give way to another if it isn't implemented appropriately. This is based on experience. Poorly implemented changes usually do go away.

It is important that teachers see the reason for a change and how and why they are expected to make it. In today's educational climate, change is a given. The diverse needs of learners require all teachers to think about their jobs differently. Every teacher deserves high-quality coaching to provide support for implementing change. Establishing the reason for change, how the change will look, and the impact this change will have on the achievement of students is the coach's primary role. Teachers have to "see through" the changes they make and how they work. The change and the change process needs to be transparent.

Reaching Agreements

The only time a change is worthwhile is when it improves the way a school or school system works. Schools and school systems only work effectively when there are sustained improvements in student achievement. When a school or school system is not performing effectively, an agreement is needed for a commitment from teachers, coaches, and administrators to work together to effect the necessary changes. Agreements are part of a trade-off. It is necessary to remove the barriers and fears that people have about change and provide the supports that will help them through the changes. As a result, the reasons and excuses for not making changes are reduced.

Agreeing about the purpose of professional development through coaching means that student learning will increase because of what each teacher learns. If teachers agree that coaching will be regular–it will occur once a week or every other week–it can also become systematic and focused. Coaching that begins with a question from the teacher and job-embedded work with a coach is followed by a professional dialogue based on the teacher's question. Student work and teacher planning will be part of the discussion. As a result of this support, the teacher can be expected to make a commitment to change in classroom practice. Everyone–teachers, administrators, and coaches–must agree to these concepts for the experience to result in increased student achievement.

Answers to the following questions can provide a measure of how successful the agreements are among coaches, teachers, and administrators.

- Is it clear that the reason for the change is the gap between our knowledge of instruction and our student achievement?
- Are the coaches and teachers clear about what needs to happen and how it will be done?
- Do the coaches and the teachers understand their responsibilities in the process?
- Are both the teachers and the coaches clear about what measures of this student achievement they will be assessing?
- Is it clear that student data will be shared consistently to show evidence of success of this process?

Establishing an Agreement

Here's an example of the steps taken at one school to reach an agreement about how coaching could be implemented.

Step 1: Sharing Student Achievement Data

The staff have come together to review the latest summative data on student achievement. The administrator notes that the data reveals that less than 25 percent of the student population has achieved proficiency on the state assessment in writing and that this level of proficiency has decreased steadily over the past two years. It is clear that writing instruction in the school needs to improve.

Step 2: Defining What Successful Students Would be Able to Do

In small groups, teachers talk about how it might look if student writing improved. What would proficient writers know and be able to do at each grade level?

Step 3: Determining Current Challenges to Improving Student Achievement

In grade-level groups, the staff brainstorms their current challenges in writing instruction. What is keeping the students from being proficient writers? What is it that they need to know?

Step 4: Establishing the Arrangements for Staff Development

The administrator shares the arrangements that have evolved for the way professional development can meet teachers' needs. He recognizes the strengths that each teacher brings to the teaching of writing and acknowledges the challenges with student writing proficiency they face as a faculty. He shares how the professional development will be designed to meet both the student achievement needs of the school and also the individual needs of the teachers. He notes that the support will be regular. All teachers will receive coaching on a weekly basis. It will be systematic; the format will be as agreed. The coaches' work alongside teachers will be focused; it will be designed around each teacher's individual challenges with writing instruction. Coaching occurs on the job, in the classroom, and in the context of the teachers' real work. It will be followed by a professional conversation. As a result, student achievement will be expected to increase.

Step 5: Reframing Teachers' Challenges into Questions

The following are examples of challenges the teachers have been raising about writing instruction:

- I don't know how to get my students to pay more attention to spelling and punctuation.
- I have trouble getting the students in my class to re-read their writing and make revisions.

- I don't have time to look at all of their writing and I find it getting away from me.
- My students aren't able to select their own topics.

The coach notes that her own challenge in writing instruction is in supporting her students in narrowing their topic selection. She finds that they seem to be picking broad topics, then losing focus as they write about them. She talks aloud in front of the staff about changing her challenge into a question. "How do I support my students in narrowing the focus of their topic?" She notes what she is currently doing in her classroom to address the issue and suggests the support that would be helpful to her. She talks about the need for someone to watch her whole group instruction when she is using her own writing to narrow her topic and give her feedback on how it seems to be working.

The coach ends by sharing her own questions and thinking by writing an action plan. She explains that the action plan is a tool that will clarify and focus her instruction.

Step 6: Identifying Roles

In small groups, the staff discusses the action plan. Each group contributes to a chart that sets out in one column the teacher's role and in the other the coach's role. Figure 7.1 illustrates.

The coach explains that when beginning, teachers often feel uncomfortable working with a coach. The coach talks about her own experience of being coached; of not knowing the

Teacher's Role	Coach's Role
Action Plan - Determine challenge - Ask question - Describe what I'm doing and make a commitment to do it - Identify where I need support	Action Plan - Review and determine where I can best provide feedback to facilitate reflection - Plan how I can provide support

Figure 7.1: The teacher's role and the coach's role

expectations and wondering if her teaching was going to be judged as right or wrong or good or bad. She also shares the questions she had about what her coach was looking for in her students' writing. She wondered what her coach was noting about her practice.

Sometimes her coach would help her in the classroom by demonstrating something for her, or posing questions to her students in a small group, or interacting with a child one-on-one. She talks about her coach sharing the notes she had taken during her observation and being surprised to see that they were just notes that focused on what she was saying and what the students were saying as it related to her question. There were questions her coach had noted; they were the questions the coach would often ask her during the dialogue.

Step 7: Focusing the Observation

The coach shares her role and responsibility when working with the teacher by adding to the chart. She then gives the teachers time to think about their role when working with the coach, which is added to the chart. This step is illustrated in Figure 7.2.

Teacher's Role	Coach's Role
Action Plan • Determine challenge • Ask question • Describe what I'm doing and make a commitment to do it • Identify where I need support Working with the Coach • Make sure my instruction at that time is around my question/challenge • Be willing to ask for help when I think I need it	Action Plan • Review and determine where I can best provide feedback to facilitate reflection • Plan how I can provide support Working with the Teacher • Focus on the teacher's question • Collect information in my notes to support the teacher • Pose questions to myself • Think about where I can best help the teacher

Figure 7.2: Adding to the roles of teacher and coach

Step 8: Establishing Roles for Instructional Dialogue

The coach notes her expectation for the instructional dialogue. She is not there to judge the quality of the lesson. She was surprised when her own coach wanted her to do a lot of the talking and that sometimes the conversation wasn't as much about the lesson as it was about the students' response to the lesson. She says she began to look forward to the opportunity to talk with someone about her teaching who knew what she was struggling with and who knew her students. Soon she found that she and her coach often worked together in the dialogue to analyze student work and plan for what would happen next.

She also says that she knew she was expected to learn something and what she learned would be evident the next time the coach came into her classroom. This was her commitment to the process. She explains that the dialogue was most helpful to her when the coach helped her work through not only what she was going to do and why but also how it would look in her practice.

It took her awhile to realize that each time she met with her coach in instructional dialogue she was expected to bring some student work. She ends by jotting down some final notes about the coach's role in dialogue and invites the teachers to talk about their role as well. This is illustrated in Figure 7.3.

Step 9: Establishing Expectations

The administrator brings closure to the meeting by once again noting where they are with student writing proficiency and where they expect to be by the end of the year. He compliments the teachers for being so open in their discussions about their role in the job-embedded professional development that is proposed. He asks if they are comfortable agreeing to the roles and responsibilities on these charts at this time–and writes the word DRAFT on the top of the chart, reminding them that this will be revisited after the process is in place. He also thanks the coach for being so open about her own experiences with coaching. He reminds the staff that this chart will be posted in the faculty lounge and teachers are invited to write their comments or questions on the chart to promote future discussion.

Teacher's Role	Coach's Role
Action Plan • Determine challenge • Ask question • Describe what I'm doing and make a commitment to do it • Identify where I need support Working with the Coach • Make sure my instruction at that time is around my question/challenge • Be willing to ask for help when I think I need it Dialogue • Talk about what I have been doing to solve my challenge • Analyze student work to see if I have been successful • Determine what I will do next and why • Ask for support in how to do it	Action Plan • Review and determine where I can best provide feedback to facilitate reflection • Plan how I can provide support Working with the Teacher • Focus on the teacher's question • Collect information in my notes to support the teacher • Pose questions to myself • Think about where I can best help the teacher Dialogue • Have an outcome—know what feedback you might provide • Listen to what the teacher says • Analyze student work • Help the teacher set expectations for what he/she will do next • Provide support, when needed, as to how this might look

Figure 7.3: Clarifying roles during dialogue

Frequently Asked Questions about the Process of Instructional Dialogue

In this book the concept of instructional dialogue involves a process that relies on using an action plan, engaging in job-embedded work and feedback, and making a commitment to change. Coaches, teachers, and administrators in schools involved in this process of coaching have many questions as they go about this work. The remainder of this chapter will address some of the more common questions asked.

How does the coach establish rapport when first working with the teacher?

There are certain criteria recommended when selecting a coach (The Learning Network® 1998). Two of the criteria are instrumental in establishing rapport with colleagues. First, the coach is selected because he or she is already respected by his or her colleagues. This often means that there is no need to establish rapport, it is already in place. Second, the coach views him- or herself as a learner, which sets the expectation that the coach and the teacher will learn together.

Rapport can be built when the coach and the teacher have informal conversations about student data. Most school districts require initial assessments on incoming students. Conversations about these assessments can help the teacher identify where he or she expects to be challenged and can be the impetus for an initial action plan. Success is a big motivator. If the initial action plans are small and achievable and result in a change in student learning, most teachers are enthusiastic about continuing the process.

For example, one fourth-grade teacher was interested in seeing if her students could self-select books for independent reading. After a conversation with the coach, she decided to meet with her students over the next week in groups of four and collect information through an informal interview about how they chose books for independent reading. She and the coach decided that they would meet in a week and the teacher would share the data she collected. During that dialogue with her coach, they identified the students who were able to select books independently, who needed a small amount of assistance, and who needed books selected for them. She reported to the coach that she felt "miles ahead" of where she had been in other years because she had this information after only the second week of school.

Teachers are appreciative of suggestions for practical application of changes. Rapport can be built quickly when the teacher feels as if he or she can go back into the classroom and quickly implement the small change resulting from the dialogue. Learning what to do is important. Learning how to put it into practice is just as important.

Finally, rapport comes when the teacher knows that coaching results in increasing student achievement. A kindergarten teacher, in her previous school, had taught her kindergarten students each letter of the alphabet in isolation. Her current group of students came to school with limited knowledge of letters and sounds. The coach encouraged her to introduce the writing process to her young students and to teach the sounds and letters through their writing. The kindergarten teacher was skeptical but said that she would agree to try this for one quarter. She and her coach used her action plans to work through her challenges. At the end of the quarter, the kindergarten teacher assessed her students on letter identification and knowledge of sounds and found that more than half of her students knew all of the letters and most of the sounds. Even though she had seen her students using letters and sounds in their writing, she was astounded to see the results when the students were asked about letters and sounds in isolation. She was convinced that the job-embedded work she did with her coach resulted in that increase in her students' achievement.

What is the role of the building administrator in a school with a coaching model?

It is vitally important for the building administrator to understand the process involved in coaching. The administrator certainly needs to support the process but more importantly needs to be involved in the process. This means the administrator must help facilitate the discussions and agreements with the entire staff. This includes scheduling time for job-embedded work with coaches and teachers. Administrators will set expectations for all staff as they relate to coaching and monitor that those expectations are being met. The difference between being passively supportive and being actively committed can make an impact on the success of the coaching initiative.

Administrators who set aside time to work alongside their coaches on a consistent basis are able to see the impact of coaching on the quality of instruction. These administrators believe that coaching is beneficial for all teachers regardless of the current quality of their instruction. They see all teachers on a continuum of learning and believe that all teachers deserve to be coached.

Finally, the role of the administrator is to monitor the impact of coaching on both teacher and student growth. This means keeping a keen eye on the link between improved student achievement data and the professional development of the school. The administrator is continually asking why. If student achievement has increased, what has caused that increase? What do teachers now know that they didn't know before, and what evidence is there of that knowledge? If student achievement has not increased, what do teachers need to know that they currently don't know, and how will the opportunities for that to happen be provided?

What are the strategies for working with resistant or reluctant teachers?

The first task is to identify what is meant by reluctant or resistant teachers. Some teachers are labeled as being resistant because they are asking questions that coaches or administrators really don't want to have asked. They are actually being reflective, but not exactly about what they might be expected to reflect on. Often, these teachers appreciate when someone listens to what they have to say and acts upon it. If resistant teachers feel as if someone is listening to what they have to say, they often become supportive of the process.

Teachers who are thought of as being reluctant have often been exposed to so many different professional development opportunities that have not been effective in improving either their classroom practice or their students' achievement that they immediately expect coaching to be the same way. They have learned from experience that if they wait long enough, this too shall pass. This is where work with student achievement is vital. All teachers want their students to succeed. With small steps, practical support, and a close eye on student growth, a coach can prove to the reluctant teachers that the changes they made have made a difference in student success.

Some teachers who are labeled as being reluctant or resistant are afraid. They have been part of an educational culture in which their work was done behind closed doors, and the only time another adult was in their classrooms was when the administrator evaluated their teaching. These teachers rarely admitted to having challenges or not knowing what to do, because to do so would be admitting ineffectiveness. Change in instruction was only expected of those who were considered to be ineffective. At that time, they considered change punitive. Making a shift to a culture where change is welcomed and expected is difficult for some people. Supporting those teachers might mean that the coach needs to provide some demonstrations of strategies that the teacher might be expected to try the following week. It might mean that the coach and the teacher do some co-teaching with small groups or individuals. Once the teacher realizes that there is nothing to fear in coaching, they are often willing participants in the process.

The most important way to support resistant, reluctant, or fearful teachers is by closely monitoring the growth of their students as a result of the changes the teachers have made. It's a rare teacher who doesn't become committed when he or she sees their growth has been the factor impacting the growth of their students.

What are the qualities of a good coach?

To provide adequate support to teachers that will improve student learning, coaches must possess the qualities of successful teachers themselves. Teachers who become coaches need a strong theoretical knowledge about their content area. They must understand how readers read; how writers write. They must know the stages through which readers and writers progress. They must be able to demonstrate the links among content areas and how those links are made through effective instruction.

In a standards-based educational system, teachers who become coaches have to have comprehensive knowledge of the expectations of state standards. They must be able to see the direct link between their knowledge of the processes of learning literacy and math and the expectations of this learning as expressed in the state standards.

They need a strong understanding of teaching and learning and how summative and formative data inform teaching and learning. Being able to apply knowledge of the processes and standards enables teachers who become coaches to evaluate the information collected about their learners. How well they do this helps them identify the strengths and next learning steps for their students.

Effective coaches are expected to support teachers in organizing the classroom as a learning environment. They are also expected to help teachers manage their diverse range of learners in a variety of instructional approaches.

Effective coaches believe that the quality of instruction is defined by the quality of learning. Teachers who provide and adjust appropriate support during instruction can see when learning is occurring.

Finally, teachers who become effective coaches expand their skills to monitor learning both when students are acquiring and applying what they have been taught.

As part of the coaches' own development, feedback should be provided as they work as teachers in the classroom with students. Coaches need support, and as their knowledge and skill in instruction increase, so does their ability to support others in a coaching role.

Coaches also need consistent feedback about the work they do in instructional dialogue and their work in facilitation. Administrators can provide valuable feedback when they are working alongside the coach. Coaches also benefit from an outside set of eyes. Someone who is not part of the day-to-day operation of the school can provide a fresh perspective to literacy coaches.

When a school faculty embarks upon job-embedded professional development, they expect success because of the support provided to teachers and the impact this will have on improving student achievement. Two things are important. The first is that the process is transparent; everyone understands their role and responsibilities. The second way of supporting success is to ensure that these roles and responsibilities are agreed to; that people understand what their job responsibilities are and what commitments they will make. Everybody will also know how success will be measured.

CHAPTER **8**

"WHY ARE WE DOING WHAT WE'RE DOING?" PRINCIPLES OF EFFECTIVE INSTRUCTIONAL DIALOGUE

There is one thing researchers agree upon: the quality of a student's school achievement is directly related to the quality of the instruction he or she receives. The purpose of instructional dialogue is to develop high-quality instruction. It follows that as teachers refine their instructional practice, student achievement will improve. Student achievement improves because teachers can link **what** they are doing to **why** they are doing it; they can more clearly describe the underlying thinking that drives their classroom practice.

Research that Supports the Concept of Instructional Dialogue

Effective instructional dialogue is driven by five basic principles supported by research:

- There are identifiable qualities linked to effective instruction
- Professional development for teachers is most effective when it occurs on the job
- A process of self-assessment leads teachers to make choices about what to focus on next in their learning
- Reflective teachers think about their work as they work
- Appropriate feedback resulting in instructional changes leads to learning gains for students.

Qualities Linked to Effective Instruction

Before teachers can be supported to improve student learning, coaches and teachers need to understand the qualities of effective instruction–the characteristics and skills teachers possess that effectively increase student achievement. Teachers whose instruction impacts student learning have certain similar qualities (Allington 2002; Darling-Hammond 1998; National Board for Professional Teaching Standards; National Education Association 2003; Pressley et al 2001; Pressley et al 2003; Rényi 1996; Stronge 2002):

- Knowledge of content standards and subject matter
- Knowledge of the stages of child and adolescent development
- Knowledge of teaching and learning and the ability to:
  - identify what students know and what they need to learn next
  - organize an environment for learning
  - manage and monitor student learning
  - provide appropriate support in order for learning to occur
- High expectations for student learning
- The ability to analyze and reflect on their practice.

When planning for instructional dialogue, a coach uses the qualities of effective instruction as a benchmark. The coach assesses the current knowledge and skill level of the teacher and determines what the teacher needs to know to increase that skill.

Job-embedded Professional Development

Joyce and Showers (2002) have been researching the impact of staff development on the learning achievement of students since 1980. They note five approaches to staff development. The first is the presentation of theory, which typically occurs in a lecture format, where the information is delivered to a passive audience; the "sit and git" of my early experiences as a teacher. The second is the demonstration or modeling of the new strategy or skill; the "sit and git" plus the model instructor. The third involves practice. The participants are provided opportunity to use what they have been taught. Finally, coaching is when the participants receive job-embedded feedback on their work.

Joyce and Showers analyzed the effectiveness of these components by looking at three outcomes:

- The acquisition of theory or knowledge (the learner can talk about what has been learned)
- The demonstration of a skill (through classroom observation or videotape)
- The application of a skill through coaching, allowing teachers to solve problems or questions that arise as they are taking on new learning.

What is interesting and no surprise to anyone in education is the difference in effectiveness of these approaches. Joyce and Showers argued that the effectiveness of these approaches is cumulative in nature. If teachers are only presented with staff development opportunities where information is delivered, then they are likely to retain little knowledge and apply none. If teachers are provided demonstrations with theory or shown how it looks in practice, they are likely to retain more knowledge and gain more skills but still apply little of what they've learned to their instruction. If teachers are provided time to practice, they retain twice the knowledge and skills, but application is minimal. Teachers who work with a more-knowledgeable other to solve problems and answer questions as they learn (such as the kind of coaching I propose in this book) transfer the knowledge and skills they attain to classroom instruction. As a result, the improved instruction has a direct impact on student learning.

Making Choices about Learning

A challenge for the coach is to make the link for the learner between what they currently know and what they need to know. This requires teachers to assess their own instruction. Sadler (1989) describes self-assessment as a sequence of two actions. The first action is the realization by the learners of a gap between what they want to know and be able to do and their current level of knowledge and skill–knowing what they don't know. The second action is the action taken by learners to close the gap and gain the knowledge and skills they need.

Added to the teachers' knowing what they don't know, research also points to the link between choice and learning. When learners have choices about what they need to learn, then learning increases (Davies 2000, 9).

The action plans described in this book provide an opportunity for learners to set out in writing what they currently know about this focus. This document offers the coach information to determine teachers' strengths. The action plan also asks teachers to describe what they are currently doing and as Preece notes, "Well formulated goals lead to action; they offer more than wishes and hopes" (1995, 37). This plan becomes the teachers' commitment to action; a commitment to change. It also provides the coach with a direction for feedback.

The coach and teacher use the action plan during instructional dialogue to keep a focus while solving the current challenge the teacher has with instruction. They come back to the questions and statements on the action plan during the dialogue to bring clarity to the discussion.

Reflection: Thinking about the Work

Highly effective teachers have sometimes been described as having some innate ability that magically allows them to teach students successfully. People are described as "born teachers," as if their professional skill is a result of their genetic makeup. Studies of such "born professionals" suggest that people who are skilled in any profession are more likely to question what they currently do and to seek opportunities to improve.

Schön explains that quality professionals know something worth knowing, are able to describe what they know, and are able to continually improve upon it through reflection-in-action. These professionals are not dismayed by the challenges they face, but allow themselves "to experience surprise, puzzlement or confusion in a situation that is uncertain or unique" (1983, 68). Schön believes this ability to question one's practice allows us the opportunity to solve our professional challenges.

Instructional dialogue puts a structure to reflection. The coach listens as the teacher talks about the challenge to instruction. Student data is shared as an opportunity for problem solving or as evidence of the effectiveness of instruction. Together the coach and teacher work to solve these challenges. The result of the reflective conversation is the opportunity for the teacher to make a change in the way classroom instruction is delivered. The outcome of this change is measured through the impact on student learning.

Feedback on Instruction Leads to Student Learning Gains

Feedback is the opportunity for a teacher to engage in reflection about his or her own practice with support from a colleague with more expertise. This assistance is structured so the teacher can solve his or her own problems. As a result, the teacher's practice changes and has a direct impact on student learning. An extensive meta-analysis of the research on formative assessment

(Black and William 1998) uncovered a key idea about feedback. Feedback only leads to learning gains when it includes guidance about how to improve (Kluger and DeNisi 1996). Typically, teachers are told what they need to do to improve instruction. Teachers are less likely to be shown what the improvement looks like and the steps needed to make that improvement.

Instructional dialogue provides opportunities for guidance in how to improve instruction. There is an expectation that teachers will talk about what they are going to change and the learning gains expected for students as a result of that change. There is also an expectation that teachers will be provided with support in how to change instruction through discussion with the coach.

It is hardly surprising that this brief review of relevant research should be consistent with what most teachers would already appreciate: the most effective professional learning comes on the job, change in practice occurs best when one thinks about why changes should be made, and effective practices are sustained through continuous support from a mentor, colleague, or coach.

As part of the professional coaching process, instructional dialogue should not be seen as something new, a fad, or fashionable. It is, as I have stated throughout this book, the kind of conversation that focuses attention on the reason why teacher and coach work together–student learning. The structured nature of the conversation that follows teacher and coach working together is concerned with not simply improving instructional practices as a measure of student learning but with how effectively students learn being the measure of instructional effectiveness. The difference may appear subtle. It is, in fact, profound.

Teachers traditionally work in a paradoxical world. On the one hand, they work alone for most of the time in a classroom. On the other hand, they are part of a school team of professionals who are only now adjusting to the demands of working together and exposing their practices and ideas to the support and scrutiny of others. I hope this book helps in the transition.

REFERENCES

Allington, Richard L. 2002. "What I've Learned about Effective Reading Instruction from a Decade of Studying Exemplary Elementary Classroom Teachers." *Phi Delta Kappan.* Volume 83, number 10, June, pages 740–747.

Armbruster, Bonnie B., Fran Lehr, and Jean Osborn. 2001. Put Reading First: The Research Building Blocks for Teaching Children to Read–Kindergarten through Grade 3. Partnership for Reading, a collaborative effort of the National Institute for Literacy, the National Institute of Child Health and Human Development, and the U. S. Department of Education, September.

Black, Paul, Chris Harrison, Clara Lee, Bethan Marshall, and Dylan William. 2003. *Assessment for Learning: Putting It into Practice.* Philadelphia, PA: Open University Press.

Black, Paul and Dylan William. 1998. "Inside the Black Box: Raising Standards through Classroom Assessment." *Phi Delta Kappan.* Volume 80, number 2, pages 139–144, 146–148.

Clarke, Shirley. 2003. *Enriching Feedback in the Primary Classroom.* London, UK: Hodder and Stoughton.

Clay, Marie M. 2000. *Running Records for Classroom Teachers.* Portsmouth, NH: Heinemann.

Darling-Hammond, Linda. 1998. "Teacher Development That Supports Student Learning." *Educational Leadership,* Volume 55, number 5, February, pages 6–11.

Davies, Anne. 2000. *Making Classroom Assessment Work.* Courtenay, British Columbia: Connections Publishing.

DiCamillo, Kate. 2000. *Because of Winn Dixie* (student edition). New York, NY: Scholastic.

Johnston, Peter. 2004. *Choice Words: How Our Language Affects Children's Learning.* York, ME: Stenhouse Publishers.

Joyce, Bruce and Beverly Showers. 1996. "The Evolution of Peer Coaching." *Educational Leadership,* Volume 53, number 6, March, pages 12–16.

Joyce, Bruce R. and Beverly Showers. 2002. *Student Achievement through Staff Development,* 3/e. Alexandria, VA: Association for Supervision and Curriculum Development.

Kluger, Avraham N. and Angelo DeNisi. 1996. "Effects of Feedback Intervention on Performance: A Historical Review, a Meta-analysis, and a Preliminary Feedback Intervention Theory." *Psychological Bulletin,* Volume 119, number 2, March, pages 254–284.

Kouzes, James M. and Barry Z. Posner. 2002. *The Leadership Challenge,* 3/e. San Francisco, CA: Jossey-Bass.

The Learning Network. 1998. "Understanding The Learning Network." Katonah, NY: Richard C. Owen Publishers, Inc.

The Learning Network Staff. 2004. *The Learning Network® Handbook for Administrators and Teacher Leaders,* 3/e. Katonah, NY: Richard C. Owen Publishers, Inc.

Mooney, Margaret E. 2003. *Books for Young Learners Teacher Resource.* Katonah, NY: Richard C. Owen Publishers, Inc.

Mooney, Margaret E. 2005. "Characteristics of Learners." In *Learning in the Content Areas: The Role of Literacy.* Katonah, NY: Richard C. Owen Publishers, Inc.

National Board for Professional Teaching Standards. www.nbpts.org

National Education Association. 2003. "Using Data about Classroom Practice and Student Work to Improve Professional Development for Educators." *The NEA Foundation for the Improvement of Education.* Spring, number 5.

O'Brien, John. 1988. "Sounds in Space" in *School Journal, Part 2, Number 1.* Wellington, New Zealand: Learning Media for Ministry of Education.

Preece, Alison. 1995. "Chapter 4: Self-Evaluation: Making it Matter." In *Assessment in the Learning Organization: Shifting the Paradigm.* Edited by Arthur L. Costa and Bena Kallick. Alexandria, VA: Association for Supervision and Curriculum Development.

Pressley, Michael, Richard L. Allington, Ruth Wharton-McDonald, Cathy Collins Block, and Lesley Mandel Morrow. 2001. *Learning to Read: Lessons from Exemplary First-Grade Classrooms.* New York, NY: Guilford Press.

Pressley, Michael, Sara E. Dolezal, Lisa M. Raphael, Lindsey Mohan, Alysia D. Roehrig, and Kristin Bogner. 2003. *Motivating Primary-Grade Students.* New York, NY: Guilford.

Rényi, Judith. 1996. "Teachers Take Charge of Their Learning: Transforming Professional Development for Student Success." The NEA Foundation for the Improvement of Education.

Sadler, D. Royce. 1989. "Formative Assessment and the Design of Instructional Systems." *Instructional Science.* Volume 18, number 2, June, pages 119–144.

Sadler, D. Royce. 1998. "Formative Assessment: Revisiting the Territory." *Assessment in Education: Principles, Policy & Practice.* Volume 5, number 1, March, pages 77–78.

Schön, Donald A. 1983. *The Reflective Practitioner: How Professionals Think in Action.* New York, NY: Basic Books.

Stronge, James H. 2002. *Qualities of Effective Teachers.* Alexandria, VA: Association for Supervision and Curriculum Development.

INDEX

About this DVD

The instructional dialogue on this DVD took place after Jan, the classroom teacher, had written an action plan and Marilyn, the coach, had read and thought about what Jan was working on. Marilyn then observed Jan's daily writing demonstration for her class. This instructional dialogue took place later that same day. Please note: Action plans do not always focus on classroom teaching; a coach may work with the teacher on any aspect of gathering student data, evaluating data, or planning for instruction.